ALSO BY EDMUND KOSTKA

Schiller in Russian Literature

Glimpses
of Germanic-Slavic Relatio
from Pushkin
to Heinrich Mann

Glimpses of Germanic-Slavic Relations from Pushkin to Heinrich Mann

EDMUND KOSTKA

Lewisburg
Bucknell University Press
London: Associated University Presses

Associated University Presses, Inc.
Cranbury, New Jersey 08512

Associated University Presses
108 New Bond Street
London W1Y OQX, England

Library of Congress Cataloging in Publication Data

Kostka, Edmund K
Glimpses of Germanic-Slavic relations from Pushkin to Heinrich Mann.

Bibliography: p.
1. Literature, Comparative—Russian and German.
2. Literature, Comparative—German and Russian.
I. Title.
PG2981.G3K6 809'.933 73-8303
ISBN 0-8387-1371-8

Abstracts or preliminary versions of the chapters included in this study have appeared in print as follows:

"Heinrich Mann and Fyodor Sologub," *Rivista di letterature moderne e comparate* XVIII (Firenze, December 1965), 245–58.

"Maksim Gorky: Russian Writer with a Western Bent," *Rivista di letterature moderne e comparate* XXIII (March 1970), 5–20.

"Blok, Schiller, and the Bolshevik Revolution," *Revue de Littérature Comparée* XXXIX (Paris, June 1965), 255–67.

"A Trailblazer of Russian Westernism: V. P. Botkin," *Comparative Literature* XVIII (Summer 1966), 211–24.

"Pushkin's Debt to Schiller," *Rivista di letterature moderne e comparate* XX (June 1967), 85–100.

"T. N. Granovsky and the Ideological Lure of the West" has not previously been published in any form and is here printed for the first time.

PRINTED IN THE UNITED STATES OF AMERICA

To
Bona, Victor, and Carlo,
with Love

Contents

Acknowledgments

The chapters on Botkin and Blok are reprinted, partially revised, by permission of *Comparative Literature,* XVIII (1966), 211–24, and *Revue de Littérature Comparée,* XXXIX (1965), 255–67.

List of Abbreviations

PMLA—*Publications of the Modern Language Association of America*
RLC—*Revue de Littérature Comparée*
SEEJ—*Slavic and East European Journal*
SEES—*Slavic and East European Studies*

Introduction

The past few decades have witnessed an unprecedented surge of public concern for the world of the Slavs accompanied by a torrent of publications on almost every aspect of Slavic history and civilization. In the presence of such an irresistible trend it may come as a surprise to find that the prolific area of Germanic-Slavic literary relations has been largely bypassed or eschewed by the explorers. As a consequence, Western scholarship has produced but an exiguous crop of contributions in this vast and vital field. Apart from the dated articles by Matl, Gorlin, and Arthur Luther, which were written in the thirties, there seem to exist no more than about a dozen major studies devoted to the problems of German-Russian literary interdependence.[1]

To be sure, meritorious efforts have been made by Marxist scholars such as Zhirmunsky, Durylin, Reissner, Ziegengeist, and Hofman.[2] But these studies tend to overemphasize the ascendancy of Russian literature over the "declining West" and, as André von Gronicka cautions in his fine book on Goethe in Russia, "generally follow officially sanctioned lines and are not always free from ideological bias." Impartial and comprehensive studies are urgently needed to reveal the complex and consequential ramifications of the German-Russian interrelationship and, in a larger context, the inspirational force of Western thought and letters for the development of Slavic civilization.

The eventful and, at times, paradoxical development of German-Russian relations originated in the early Middle Ages. The impact of the Western heritage on the process of civilizing Russia can hardly be overestimated. Even Marxist scholars do not deny that it constituted "a decisive characteristic of the evolution of Russia."[3] In this context it may seem desirable and fruitful to view Russian literature in terms of its creative indebtedness to its West-European neighbors.

One of the first Germans to envision a cultural synthesis between the values of the East and the West was the philosopher G. W. Leibniz. His plan for the development of cultural and commercial relations, which he submitted to Peter the Great, was not carried out at the time but it provided a blue-print for future cooperation. In the year 1630 the poet Paul Fleming was sent to Russia by the Duke of Holstein in order to explore new channels of trade. Fleming's poems on Moscow, the Volga River, and the Caucasian Mountains have remained as the poetic harvest of his adventurous journey.

At the beginning of the eighteenth century the German Pietists established contacts between the educational centers of the two countries. As a result, many Russian students flocked to the University of Halle, but also to Göttingen and Leipzig. The efficient trade organization of the Francke Foundation provided the Russian reading public with the most significant West-European periodicals and books. To please the courtiers at St. Petersburg, the fashionable actress Caroline Neuber was imported from Germany, together with her entire company, followed in 1745 by the equally renowned theater stars Sophie Schröder and K. E. Ackermann. Their highly pleasing performances led to the establishment of the first Russian theater company at St. Petersburg in 1756.[4]

Toward the end of the eighteenth century the poet J. G. Herder became the founder of Western Slavic philology, the science of the Slavic languages. In his fundamental work, *Ideen zur Philosophie der Geschichte der Menschheit* (1784–91), he dedicated an entire chapter to the evolution and destiny of the Slavic race. Foreshadowing the tenets of the budding Romantic movement, Herder gave a highly idealized picture of the Slavs. Other German writers such as Klinger, G. Forster, and Seume, in this respect more fortunate than Herder, were able to travel extensively in Russia. Their impressions and experiences induced them to grow increasingly critical of the Russian feudal system and of autocracy, and they did not hesitate to voice disapproval in their diaries and other writings. Very sharp social criticism came from the pen of Johann Georg Forster, recently rediscovered and claimed as a "revolutionary writer" by Marxist scholarship.

A separate study would be needed to deal with the history of German-Russian intermarriage between noble, aristocratic, and royal families. Suffice it to mention that Empress Catherine II, the wife of Tsar Peter III, was a née Princess of Anhalt-Zerbst, and that also the wife of the last Russian Tsar, Nicholas II, had come to St. Petersburg from Germany. Family connections on the level of royalty were bound to have above all diplomatic and political importance whereas lesser relationships often acted as catalysts precipitating a literary reaction. Thus, after the inauguration of intimate dynastic ties between Weimar and St. Petersburg (the heir apparent of Weimar, Karl Friedrich, married the daughter of Tsar Paul I, Maria Pavlovna), it was almost a matter of course that also Goethe and Schiller should establish a relationship with Russian officialdom and culture. In fact, both Schiller's *Demetrius* and *Die Huldigung der Künste* owe their genesis to occurrences provided by the course of Russian history. As for Goethe, his manifold official and literary associations with the world of the Slavs have been the subject of detailed studies by such authors as Zhirmunsky and von Gronicka.

A word must be said about the impact of German philosophy upon the Russian mind which has been unusually consequential. In the early eighteenth century we witness the rapid spread of Jakob Böhme's philosophical mysticism throughout Russia followed by the enthusiastic reception of Schelling, Hegel, and Marx by the Russian intelligentsia a hundred years later.[5] Other German philosophers who have left an imprint on the Russian intellectual development are J. G. Fichte and Max Stirner.

An important figure in German-Russian interrelations was Nikolay Karamzin, who carried on a lively correspondence with the Swiss theologian J. K. Lavater. During his stay in Western Europe (1789–90) he paid his respects to Kant, Herder, Wieland, and several other German literary celebrities. Russian-German cooperation reached a high point during the national Wars of Liberation (1813–15), which were fought on the European continent to free the peoples from the Napoleonic yoke. The treaty of Tauroggen and the creation of the Russian-German Legion are regarded as historic landmarks not only in the communist part of Germany but also in the Soviet Union.

Even more important as an intermediary was the poet and translator V. A. Zhukovsky. His masterly renderings of Schiller's ballads and his romanticized version of *The Maid of Orleans* proved so successful that many Russians came to regard Schiller as a national Russian author. In consequence, there was hardly a member of the Russian intelligentsia who did not fall under the spell of the German poet at one time or another.

The vogue of Schiller (and other Western writers such as Shakespeare, Goethe, and Byron), continued throughout the first half of the nineteenth century with undiminished intensity. In the early 1830s the University of Moscow became a prominent center of Westernism due to the activities of Stankevich and Herzen. The circle of Stankevich focused its attention on the exploration of German philosophy and literature while the circle of Herzen was devoted to the study of socio-political questions. About 1840 the two circles merged under the motto of progress and free social institutions bringing thus into existence the movement of the Westerners. Botkin, Bakunin, Granovsky, and Belinsky, among others, were influential members of this movement. Struggling against their ideological adversaries, the Slavophiles, and against Tsarist autocracy, they made through their writings a great contribution to the development of Russian civilization.[6]

For a short time also Lermontov was connected with the romantic wisdom-lovers of the Stankevich circle and exposed to their heated debates about German thought and letters. Before long he fell in love with the poetry of Schiller and used him as a model in his own dramatic production.

In the second half of the nineteenth century German-Russian cultural relations were greatly intensified by the rising fame of Turgenev, Tolstoy, and Dostoyevsky. Many German writers, for instance Holz, Schlaf, and Paul Ernst, were attracted by the socio-critical and ethical tone of the Russians. Others, particularly Nietzsche, fell under the spell of Dostoyevsky's psychoanalytical approach.

After the first world war a tidal wave of enthusiasm for Russian literature, especially that of Dostoyevsky, swept across Western Europe. In its wake engaging biographies and memoirs of the "holy sinner" appeared in print, mainly in Germany, kindling the imagination of writers, critics, and the public at large.[7] Almost overnight Dostoyevsky's name was raised to the status of a symbol by the most diverse schools and factions. Thus, both the conservatists and the radicals inscribed his "creed" on their militant banners while the disciples of Freud appropriated his personality and the characters of his works to corroborate their psychoanalytical assumptions.

The rich field of Gerhart Hauptmann's affinities with

Russian literature has not yet been explored in detail; but some Soviet critics, such as T. Motylyova, contend that many important works (for example, *Die Weber, Michael Kramer, Rose Bernd,* and *Emanuel Quint*), are heavily indebted to Dostoyevsky and Tolstoy.[8]

Many other German authors felt the ascendancy of the great Russian masters. The list includes, just to mention a few, Fontane, Rilke, Kafka, and the brothers Mann. Amidst the host of contemporary writers the name of Heinrich Böll seems destined to attain a conspicuous place in the history of German-Russian literary relations.[9]

The present study is offered as a small contribution to the field of German-Russian cultural interdependence. Each of the six chapters deals with the critical or creative reception of German literature by Russian writers or vice versa. The common link which endeavors to unite the components is provided by the comparative theme. As for the method, it may be termed, accordingly, comparative-historical and ideational-typological. Such an approach implies certain tangible advantages. For instance, it can help to uncover hidden facets of a writer's personality or lead to unremembered springs of his artistic inspiration. These and other advantages are forever lost to the student of one individual, "national" literature.

I would like to stress that the comparative theme or leitmotiv should not be viewed as the only bond between the various parts of this study. In a certain sense and to a certain degree, I aimed at making visible that which is invisible by its very nature: the ageless idea of the oneness of the human spirit. How fascinating to trace the secret filaments of spiritual affinity by which Pushkin is linked to Schiller, Botkin to Beethoven, Gorky to Ibsen, and Heinrich Mann to Fyodor Sologub. What an iridescence of creative impulses, spiritual attitudes, aesthetic postulates and ideological assumptions. Yet at the same time, what an impressive community of European humanistic culture in spite of deep-rooted historical differences. These vigorous representatives of the Western spirit, which is just a geographical variety of the universal human spirit, sometimes loved and sometimes hated each other, but above and beyond their antagonisms, they always were able and willing to learn from one another. An analysis and perceptive assessment of their relationships and interdependence can go far to elucidate certain facets of their impressive achievements though it will never explain or exhaust the mystery of their poetic drive and urge of artistic creation.

1

A Literary Quandary: Fyodor Sologub and Heinrich Mann

"Power politics cannot induce me to hate Russia for there is too much in my cultural background that I owe to Russian thought" ("Meine Zeit"). In these words which recall Goethe's remark to Eckermann of March 14, 1830, Thomas Mann acknowledged his indebtedness to Russia in no uncertain terms. In corroboration of the writer's own testimony a number of essays and two major studies dealing with his relation to Russian literature have appeared in print in recent years.[1] Of course, these efforts have not exhausted the complex problem of Thomas Mann's affinities with the world of Russian letters, but they have established a foundation on which future investigators can safely build.

Turning from Thomas Mann to Heinrich Mann it is easy to see that the springs of his literary inspiration flow from the opposite direction. Whereas the works of his brother literally teem with references to Russia, Heinrich Mann's pronouncements on the same subject are significantly scarce. And small wonder, for his literary guiding stars sparkled on the horizon of the Western firmament: "There is hardly a German poet since Heinrich Heine who has attained a more intimate relationship to French literature and history than he [Heinrich Mann]. His life and his works are insolubly linked with France" (A. Kantorowicz, *Die Zeit,* March 19, 1965). What is more, in his trenchant autobiography, *Ein Zeitalter wird besichtigt,* Heinrich Mann himself clearly characterizes his education and spiritual development: "My education was French as well as German . . . Directly or indirectly we derive nourishment from the word of France."

No question, statements such as these are richly substantiated by sober and solid facts, that is by the biography and literary production of the German writer. Yet there emerges at least one major work by Heinrich Mann, *Professor Unrat* (1905), which bears a perplexing resemblance to the great novel of a *Russian* poet and romancier, Fyodor Sologub's *The Little Demon* (1892–1902). Its protagonist Peredonov (a proverbial figure in Russian literature), spreads fear and terror among his unfortunate students like his colleague Unrat. Furthermore, both novels envelop the reader in a very peculiar atmosphere of individualism, aestheticism, nihilism, and sexual perversion. Not only the established order of society but the reality and validity of life itself are challenged in the name of beauty, indicted before the tribunal of humanity, and inescapably condemned. The dreary melancholy of isolated existence assumes in both works a highly significative symbolic dimension which is suggestive of the hopeless melancholy of human existence.

To be sure, these are general similarities. But the parallelism goes much farther and much deeper, extending into the sphere of artistic and psychological details. In the ninth chapter of *The Little Demon* one comes across the following passage:

> Peredonov walked through wretched streets and along shabby houses, beneath a strange sky, on the impure and powerless earth. An indeterminate feeling of anguish weighed

> upon his soul–and there was no comfort to him in the sublime and no consolation in earthly things. As always, he gazed at the world with dead eyes like a demon who consumes himself in gloomy loneliness–full of grief, and fear, and sorrow.[2]

This Russian schoolteacher is an impure creature with a dull mind and with sinister instincts, a threatening bundle of incalculable impulses. Whatsoever he touches with his unclean hands turns into slime and filth. He hates purity, he loathes cleanliness with all the fibers of his nature: "He lustily laughed with pleasure when something was soiled in his presence."[3] His students shake with fear the moment he enters the classroom, for he is a petty tyrant—like Unrat. The most bizarre whims pop up in his confused mind. In one respect, however, he remains unchangeable: in his furious antipathy for neatness and order. Students who catch his eye owing to their "excessive" tidiness immediately become the victims of a most insidious and relentless persecution. Neatness was incomprehensible and suspicious to him—as incomprehensible and suspicious as Lohmann's polished fingernails and snow-white cuffs to Professor Unrat.

Tyrannical individuals have no friends. Peredonov "did not like people and thought of them only in connection with his own needs and desires."[4] Dislike of man had taken possession also of Unrat's mind. The whole town seemed to him a hostile camp, the whole community "a rebellious class of fifty thousand students" who instead of saluting grinned at him in open defiance and sneeringly shouted his offensive nickname. "He had never experienced genuine friendship."[5] Even his passion for the actress Fröhlich was nothing but a late, unnatural sensuality, "a sensuality wrung from his dried up body by dint of slow subterraneous seduction which in a violent and unnatural flare-up had changed his life and driven his mind to extremes."[6] Certainly, Peredonov knew even less of love and friendship than his colleague Unrat. Peredonov floated through life like a mollusk, a jellyfish, an amoeba. His relationship to Varvara hinged upon the satiation of carnal appetites. He thought nothing of abusing her with kicks and filthy words or of spitting into her face.[7] Peripheral characters are continually in danger of being hurled out of the circle of normality and human decency. Grotesque comicality and freakish mania are their pitiful destiny. Weird phantoms and fixed ideas oppressed Peredonov's eccentric mind. He saw mortal enemies not only in his terrorized students but also in his superiors and colleagues. He even dreaded his mistress Varvara by whom he continually feared to be insidiously poisoned. In every doorway and corner he fancied a spy keeping a watchful eye on him although he himself was a spy and an informer. Like Unrat he spied with morbid eagerness on his students, particularly on the quiet and industrious Sasha Pylnikov. Haunted by the unbearable idea that Sasha was not a boy but a girl in disguise, he went to extremes to have him expelled from school on ground of corruption of morals. Yet the most dismal thing in Peredonov's life was a loathsome specter accompanying relentlessly each of his steps—the grey and slimy Nedotykomka. Gradually, his fear of this intangible and ubiquitous specter increased to such a degree that it became an obsession which ultimately degenerated into frenzied insanity.

Similar phantoms and fixed ideas undermined and eventually destroyed the life of Professor Unrat. Well knowing that he was hated and feared by his students, he treated them as "archenemies" who must be "caught" and prevented from reaching the "goal of the class."[8] Just as Peredonov played ugly tricks on Sasha Pylnikov, so Professor Unrat played tricks on his student Lohmann. With wretched stubbornness he sought "to remove *this* student, to protect human society from *this* infectious individual."[9] With grim determination, he spent night after night in the dressing room of a sailors' tavern in order to keep Lohmann away from the actress Fröhlich. Like Peredonov, he fancied that he was pursued by an eerie and uncanny specter that sneeringly grinned at him out of corners and niches. His heart pounding wildly, he stopped on the street, held his breath and listened. "The vague forms in the shade stirred up fear and trepidation in his soul; every street corner had a ghastly appearance."[10] Even the moon seemed to make faces at him: "a sneering eye that immediately closed its lid again so that it was impossible to 'prove' it had mocked him."[11] Filled with a gloomy foreboding, he anticipated the day the specter would appear before him in flesh and blood to press its horrible fingers around his throat. And suddenly—as he had anticipated and dreaded—the specter emerged and reached for him and for his prized possessions. Unrat stood petrified. Insanity surged into his brain: he turned into a spider, into a cat with "crazy eyes over which colored drops of sweat were running and with foam on his trembling jaw."[12] This was his end, "The End of a Tyrant," as the subtitle of the novel reads. The fiendish Nedotykomka had won another victory.

The scene of Heinrich Mann's novel is a small German town, a provincial town inhabited by dull, malicious, gossiping, corrupted burghers. It is with exquisite skill that the author distributes the social motif among his numerous characters. The aristocracy is represented by von Ertzum, a young man of good manners and an amazing naïveté who stolidly believes in the innocence and virginity of a tavern singer. The only remarkable thing in him is his face which, according to Lohmann, looks exactly like a "boozy moon." The representatives of justice are benevolent gentlemen wringing their hands in despair over the foolishness of Lohmann and his friends. Why had these young men not come voluntarily to the authorities and confessed to their juvenile pranks? "The public prosecutor would have avoided any publicity and scandal."[13]

Among the members of the middle class we meet drunkards like the port inspector Kieselack, religious fanatics like the shoemaker Rindfleisch, philistines in the disguise of free-thinkers like Professor Unrat. Both Unrat and Peredonov embody the type of the hypocritical philistine who, although unbelieving, still insists on obedience, religion, and morality in his subordinates. Being despots by nature, they instinctively know how to maintain authority, keep slaves, rule the unenlightened rabble.[14]

High school teacher Richter, a notorious have-not, represents the model of an unscrupulous place-hunter striving to make a career via a rich marriage (a parallel to Marfa in *The Little Demon*) "in a distinguished family to which ordinarily high school teachers did not raise their eyes."[15]

Duplicity, deceit, and calculation prevail also in the lower middle classes. The dressmaker is scandalized by Unrat's love Affair with the actress Fröhlich but prudently waits until he has paid the bill for his lover's dresses before giving vent to her moral indignation. Yet the dressmaker is not an exception. The whole town seems to be infected by the virus of hypocrisy and ignorance. While Peredonov represents the shocking example of a teacher who consistently shuns research and reading, there are also in Heinrich Mann's town numerous Peredonovs—wealthy and influential citizens—who have never taken a book into their hands. To complete the picture, one may add the adultress Dora Breetpoot, the card-sharper Kieselack junior, the bankrupt wine merchant Lorenzen, and the fraudulent consul Breetpoot.

Among these mediocre and philistine characters Unrat stands out like a tower, the heroic-grotesque figure of a petty bourgeois struggling for self-liberation. No question, from the very beginning he is not only a crazy philologist but also:

> an Attila, a scourge, a phantom bordering upon unreality before whom the whole town trembles in its foundations. Yet while struggling with the town this phantom turns into a great destiny which breaks down all moral and social bounds. It outgrows the small town and touches a world where adventure, human arbitrariness and licentiousness constitute the only

> standards. The simple character of the town dissolves in the person of Professor Unrat into unlimited possibilities. The great world grins into the small town changing people and their destinies, undermining lives, crushing characters, destroying traditions.[16]

The type of the demonized small bourgeois is by no means a sporadic phenomenon in the literary production of Heinrich Mann. Through many of his novels goes like a red thread his fervent "interest for the 'bad': demoniacal characters who are obsessed by themselves."[17] The same is true of the works of Fyodor Sologub. Time and again the Russian writer depicts demoniacal figures in his stories, plays, and novels. The names of Peredonov, Login, Trirodov are links in a long chain of satanic characters.

The scene of the novel *The Little Demon* is likewise a small town. The hopeless triviality of life, however, knows no frontiers; and melancholy, corruption, anguish, and vice weigh heavily on the souls of the Russian burghers. The figure of Peredonov constitutes the physical focus of all the invisible and ineffable miseries of Russian provincial life. The demon embodied in Peredonov is, accordingly, a little demon that has nothing in common with the great spirit of negation and doubt by whom Faust and Ivan Karamazov had been tormented. The element of the little demon is not motion and activity—but stagnation, rottenness, putrefaction. The province is its uncontested domain—it is the grey specter of provincial paltriness which is diffused in the whole world. Peredonov's town teems with individuals infected by its poisonous breath: ruthless place-hunters like the aristocrat Veriga, mendacious intriguers like the concubine Varvara, shameless cynics like Rutilov, bawdy procurers like Vershina. . . . The tangible reality of life—brought to extreme expression—dissolves here all of a sudden and falls into a maze of fateful contradictions. Far away from truth, goodness, and beauty, it degenerates into chaos, horror, and insanity; and both the author and his reader are precipitated into a nightmare of diabolic dreams.

An uncanny atmosphere of hopelessness pervades the streets and houses of the town. Not human beings with human faces live here but creatures with snouts, trunks, and mugs which reveal the triumph of evil and bestiality. Very appropriately a critic has observed that *The Little Demon* is "more appalling than the roaring of a beast of prey."[18] The children alone are innocent and pure in this world of vulgarity. The adults, on the other hand, belong with bodies and souls to the terrible demon. The dance of the drunkards in Peredonov's room—doubtless a symbol of the grotesque and demoniacal dance of life—reveals this in an utterly unequivocal and shocking way. To be sure, the beastly scenes depicted by the writer are not at all just feverish dreams or infernal nightmares. "Real life," a countryman of Sologub observes, "is a million times more dreadful than all his nightmarish dreams."[19] Both Peredonov and Unrat perish as victims of this atrocious reality of life, of its ghastly and piggish *danse macabre*—and terrible seems no longer the madness of Peredonov and Unrat but the madness of human life.

Is there no way out of the slush of baseness and triviality, no way out of the grotesque realm of ghosts and specters? As a matter of fact, there are characters in both novels that seem to contradict the assumption that the "Peredonovshchina" represents a disease of universal dimensions. In Heinrich Mann's novel the student Lohmann is such an exceptional character. In *The Little Demon* Sasha Pylnikov and Ludmila Rutilova embody the antithesis to small-town banality. All three of them are endowed with qualities their neighbors do not have and by which they are raised above the dullness of everyday life. The difference consists in their natural and uncorrupted capacity for abandoning themselves to dreams of love and beauty and in their stoical willingness to accept the suffering resulting from their dreams. Thus Sasha Pylnikov has become enamored of beautiful Ludmila Rutilova who is far older than he himself, and Lohmann is deeply in love with Dora Breetpoot, who has left behind her the prime of her years. In both cases the sentiment in question may be characterized as a pure and childish love which contrasts with the brutal sensuality of the other characters. As for Ludmila, she probably appears in an even more enchanting light than Sasha Pylnikov or Lohmann. Disillusioned and discontented with life, she transforms the world according to her own needs and dreams endowing it with attributes it does not possess at all but which, nevertheless, are extant in the dream world she has created in her imagination. Rapturous love and aesthetic ecstasy help her turn her dreary life into a beautiful fairy tale.

A dreamer and creator of fairy tales (in the Sologubian sense) lives in the student Lohmann. He is the only representative of the spirit in Heinrich Mann's novel, the type of the eternally dissatisfied ponderer—a sort of decadent Faust. He loves the things "because of the reminiscences they produce, the love of women only on account of the bitter loneliness that follows, happiness at most for the sake of the choking longing it leaves in one's throat."[20] But he is more than just a dreamer—he is also the author of exuberant love poems. One night, overwhelmed by the throbbing of his yearning heart, he ardently kissed the door of Dora Breetpoot's house. Later, in a fit of despair, he hid a rifle in his father's warehouse to shoot himself in case his agonizing secret was discovered. Yet no one ever discovered it and "Lohmann could keep playing to himself and experiencing the wild chastity, the voluptuous bitterness, the timid, conceited, comforting world-disdain of his seventeen years. . . ."[21] As he grew older he arrived at a more objective perception of the world—and fear of life and its realities suddenly laid hold of him. The dreamer, "touched by the spirit" and imbued with the romanticism of Heinrich Heine, collided with the hard facts of every-day life and experienced the shock of awakening. His observing eyes soon saw through the comedy of human existence; disenchantment, weariness, and bitterness filled him "up to the neck." Empty and charred, without a spark in his heart, he finally went to the house of the actress Rosa Fröhlich. The specter of the "Peredonovshchina" had vanquished him.

There is poignant melancholy at the bottom of these seemingly comical novels, a profound sorrow at the utter helplessness of man in the face of an invincible enemy. Man, according to this gloomy philosophy, is but a pitiable prisoner—an hostage of implacable and monstrous life, and the only thing left to him is despair. Such is the reaction of vanquished Lohmann when he finally realized "what life had made of him."[22] God does not exist in this world of demoniacal paltriness, and even if he did exist he would not have any use for the wretched human worms:

> I am the God of the riddle world,
> The entire world is but my dream.[23]

However, from this self-deification does not necessarily follow the negation of God in an absolute sense. It may be a paradox, yet Sologub—like Ivan Karamazov—rejects not God but the world created by God. In this respect, the parallel to the religious and socio-political views of the German writer is far-reaching. Needless to say, neither Heinrich Mann nor Fyodor Sologub were philosophers in the strict sense of the word, nor did they dream of elaborating a philosophical system of their own. But a metaphysical aura pervades their works and an agonizing melancholy lurks at the bottom of their concepts and ideas—it is the same ominous melancholy by which their Unrats and Peredonovs are driven to despair and madness.

Nevertheless, in the presence of heavy odds the writer attempts to escape from the fiendish triviality of life into a realm of magic beauty. "Beauty" is Sologub's occult formula by means of which he endeavors to exorcise the grey specter of the "Nedotykomka." In the economy of his novel, the figure of the sensuous pagan Ludmila represents thus the counterpoise to the gloomy philistine Peredonov. Like the Duchess of Assy, Ludmila dreams of the "supple bodies of a beautiful race," of "marvellous islands of pleasure where people without want and almost without yearning may forget that there is a government, a church, and a suffering humanity."[24] At last, Ludmila finds the embodiment of her longing for beauty in handsome Sasha Pylnikov whom she surrounds with a cult of aesthetic ecstasies:

> Sasha and Ludmila are alone. Ludmila dressed him up as a barefoot fisher boy—with a rose-colored silk frock—, made him lie down on her low couch and squatted on the rug at his naked legs, bare-footed and dressed with nothing but a shirt. The vestments and Sasha's body she sprinkled with fragrant perfumes—a heavy, prudish odor of herbs filled the room like the sluggish odor of a valley girded by mountains and covered with magic flowers.
>
> Large multi-colored glass pearls glittered on her neck, chiseled bracelets of gold tinkled on her wrists, and her beautiful body smelled of iris—an odor inciting, and languorous, and sensual, pregnant with the atmosphere of hidden ponds that instilled drowsiness and sweet indolence into the limbs.
>
> Languishing and sighing she gazed at his tanned face, his bluish-black lashes, and his eyes which were dark as the night. She leaned her head against his naked knees and her blond curls caressed his sun-bronzed skin. She covered Sasha's body with kisses, and from its strange and powerful aroma which was mingled with the scent of young skin she almost lost her senses.[25]

It was Ivan Razumnik who justly characterized the Ludmila-Sasha episode as "the central and cardinal point of the whole novel."[26] Without this episode, without this triumph over triviality and madness, the reader of *The Little Demon* would suffocate in a morass of bestiality and horror. But even the positive characters in the novel are corroded by the venomous breath of the all-embracing "Peredonovshchina." Romantic Ludmila, for instance, does not seem averse to making a "good match" by marrying that paragon of triviality, Peredonov, whom she despises from the bottom of her heart. Similarly, Lohmann, who looks down at the world with the superior air of a philosopher and dreamer, refuses to acquiesce in the theft of his property. In the end—although with numerous scruples—he resorts to a completely unromantic device: he reports the theft to the police.

It is easy to sit in judgment over a notorious evildoer. At the first glance, both Peredonov and Unrat appear thoroughly guilty and worthy of punishment. The matter looks different, however, if considered *sub specie aeternitatis.* Then it becomes evident how cruelly they were treated by their fellow citizens, how circumstances and conditions implacably conspired to bring about their madness and destruction. There was no one in the whole town who understood Peredonov. No one understood his secret longing, his hidden dreams—no one understood his shuddering at the blear-eyed "Nedotykomka." Yet even Peredonov had his Dulcinea and yearned after a higher life with all the strength of his sluggish spirit:

> Yes, also Peredonov strove for truth in accordance with the universal law of all conscious life—and this striving filled him with agony. He himself did not realize that also he, as all men, was striving for truth and therefore there was so much melancholy in his restlessness. He was unable to find the truth for himself and became entrapped—and went to ruin.[27]

He went to ruin in a rage of evil and madness. Nevertheless, it was argued that his infernal agony cries out to be justified before the world in the name of love and justice. "To hell 'satire' and 'embodiment of evil' if a living human being—the past, the future Ardalyon Peredonov—carries such an unparalleled, such a hopeless burden of calamity upon his shoulders."[28] An invisible hand compressed his throat—and he could not defend himself and nothing was left to him but the agony of strangulation. Yet also Peredonov had a heart, and is not a human heart greater than human justice? From this viewpoint his calamity is desperately unjust. The tears of a tortured child must be justified because we must know: why? what for? But likewise "every slimy tear of Peredonov must be justified, every shudder at the horrible "Nedotykomka," every kick with the heel in his face he 'justly' receives from a respectable person, every shriek and wail in the madhouse where they will mercilessly lock him up."[29] Beyond the limits of conventional justice the concepts of guilt, responsibility, and punishability evaporate into thin air. "We do not judge Peredonov any longer—we cover him; and after having covered him we ask the question: How did his creator dare to create him and how will he account for his creature?"[30]

It is not difficult to perceive that also Professor Unrat may be seen as a victim of human society and circumstances. There was little more in his pitiful life than loneliness, hate, and despair. Mocked and persecuted by the entire town, he became a social outcast like his colleague Peredonov. No one understood his secret fears and ardent longings—no one except the whimsical dreamer Lohmann who occasionally took compassion on the wretched old man, "compassion and even a sort of reserved sympathy for this lonely enemy of all mankind. . . ."[31] The solitary rainbow-chaser Lohmann intuitively understands that the solitary anarchist Unrat "is also only human" and that "one should not expect any meanness of him beyond his strength."[32] But even Lohmann's penetrating eyes did not reach the last corners of the tyrant's soul. What could he know of its desperate flights over abysses, its agonizing incineration, its desolate loneliness? Neither he nor anyone else was able to divine the fearful scope of Unrat's destiny: to suffer infernal torments because of himself and because of society, to cremate ungratified longings in his own aching heart, to bury "screams of agony in the depths of his own bosom."[33] Unrat's attempt to build a new life in the old environment propels him into conflict with established society. He fights back ferociously—but he is alone and the odds are against him. The isolated rebel is bound to succumb in the unequal struggle, "a moving, heroic figure surrounded by irony and melancholy, an erratic rock of a man, representative of all enslaved and proscribed creatures."[34] Like Peredonov, he is a ruthless little tyrant—but also tyrants are haunted by hopes and fears and tormented by agonies. "He who exercises power is its slave no less than he who suffers from it. The tyrant (who is not a tyrant!) suffers from mankind as mankind from him."[35] He was called "Unrat" by his students. Perhaps his destiny was in his name, for "no one can fight forever against such a name."[36]

In his Foreword to the second edition of *The Little Demon* Sologub makes the following statement:

> I was not obliged to write from my imagination. Everything anecdotal, episodical, and psychological in my novel is based upon most careful observation and I had enough 'nature' for my novel in my immediate surroundings . . . This novel is an ingeniously polished mirror . . . a mirror which is not a distorting mirror.[37]

The realistic character of *The Little Demon* is thus confirmed by Sologub himself. But there are many elements in this novel which tend to invalidate the claim of realism put forward by the author. A magic veil of mystery envelops the novel, and an attentive reader cannot fail to see through its deceptive, pseudo-objective tone and paraphernalia. Behind the realistic façade there lurk myth, and legend, and the agonizing riddles of the Russian sphinx. Unexpectedly, the writer turns into a seer and priest: from his lips flow ecstatic words of wisdom. Socrates or an ancient oracle might have uttered similar words. No wonder then that Sologub was paralleled with the venerable figures of cryptic antiquity:

> Socrates is an oracle. His prose is not realism but vapor intoxicating the senses; and his poetry is an eternal, agonizing enigma like the oracles of Pythia. In Sologub's prose too vibrates a mysterious music the portent of which to unriddle is denied both to him and his readers.[38]

No matter how ingeniously one may try to analyze the phenomenon called Ardalyon Peredonov, there will remain an insoluble sediment of doubt and enigma in the end. A riddle is likewise the nightmarish "Nedotykomka" although some have attempted to interpret it as a hallucination born in the morbid mind of Peredonov. One cannot deny that aspects of reality are extant in this remarkable novel. Sologub's Russia, however, surpasses simple "reality"—it is a fantastically enchanted, a hyperbolically distorted reality that comes to life under his magic pen. "The Russian town depicted with such a perplexing authenticity turns into a symbol—not the town but life itself creates characters like Peredonov, life as such, the dragon that scorches everything with its fiery breath."[39]

In the eyes of many *The Little Demon* ranks as a classic, and there are some who extol it as "the best and greatest Russian novel since *The Brothers Karamazov.*"[40] Not without reason its author was dubbed "the completer of the Decadence who expressed what Verlaine had not been able to express."[41] And indeed, both form and content reveal that *The Little Demon* may lay claim to being a characteristic specimen of that movement, embodying its most distinctive elements and features. Thus, for instance, individualism is represented by the figure of Peredonov, symbolism by the gruesome "Nedotykomka," flamboyant eroticism by the Ludmila-Sasha episode. The sultry atmosphere of the novel, on the other hand, is but a faithful reproduction of the stifling Russian atmosphere in the years preceding the outbreak of the first world war. Sologub's abhorrence of living in such an atmosphere, his caustic skepticism, and his attempt to escape into a magic world of beauty have found poetic expression in the disturbing, ecstatic, shocking pages of *The Little Demon.*

It is in the same period of time, at the turn of the century, that we observe the unfolding of the talents of Heinrich Mann with little distance in the chronology:

> The embers of the world and the age, the unconfoundable age of the declining nineteenth century and the European world, kindled the poetic furor in his soul. Out of these times and this world emerged his figures—and he arranged them in his chosen field of vision where he proposed to represent his subjects.[42]

He laid the scene for the unfolding of a bizarre human destiny in the crooked lanes and gable houses of his home town. "After all his preceding experiences and trials, attainments and perceptions, it could not possibly become an idyl."[43] And no mistake—far from being an idyl, *Professor Unrat* vies with *The Little Demon* in virulent satire on the German variety of "Peredonovshchina." But as in *The Little Demon,* the macabre specter of disaster and insanity lurks behind the thin layer of comedy and grotesqueness. Unrat's crass individualism and eroticism afford another parallel and, of course, there is the same metaphysical symbolism which transposes the work to a sphere of timeless universality. As a result, even critics hostile to Heinrich Mann have grudgingly given their praise to the novel. His admirers, on the other hand, have not hesitated to elevate Professor Unrat to the rank of "one of the greatest figures in German literature."[44]

Apart from their literary value, both novels hold considerable interests as psychological testimonials of European middle-class life in the period of its prosperity and expansion. Commenting upon the race of men responsible for the accumulation of so much material wealth, Heinrich Mann once regretfully observed: "Our generation is not called to create beauty—it is solely capable of yearning and languishing for it."[45] But it was Sologub who courageously put his finger on the sore spot of frail and imperfect humanity:

> The image of Peredonov represents the universal human inclination for evil—the almost unselfish tendency of a perverse human soul to deviate from the common course of cos-

> mic life guided by an almighty Will. And while it takes vengeance on the world for its own agonizing loneliness it brings malice and horrors into the world, it mutilates existent reality and soils the beautiful dreams of mankind.[46]

Sologub here refers to Peredonov but the analogy to Professor Unrat is at close quarters and utterly suggestive.

The juxtaposition of the two novels engenders a number of tantalizing questions. Surely, the parallels and affinities —some of which have been pointed out—speak their own challenging language and a query regarding the originality of Heinrich Mann's *Professor Unrat* might not seem inappropriate under these circumstances. Since *The Little Demon* was completed in 1902 (three years earlier than *Professor Unrat*), a direct or indirect influence on the novel of the German writer would be entirely conceivable. Yet it appears that Heinrich Mann lacked even a minimal proficiency in the intricacies of the Russian language. Nevertheless, he may have heard about Sologub and his novel from his brother Thomas Mann during their sojourn in Italy. It was in fact in the summer of 1898 that Thomas Mann turned with enthusiasm to the study of Russian literature, a study which resulted in the publication of a *Russian Anthology.*[47]

For the time being one has to lean on circumstantial evidence to support the thesis of Heinrich Mann's indebtedness to Sologub's *The Little Demon.* Perhaps the surprising similarities between *Professor Unrat* and *The Little Demon* are purely accidental, perhaps it is just a striking case of literary parallelism. Maybe so, but then it looms as a case of parallelism which borders on telepathy and magic. Then, to use an expression by Vyacheslav Ivanov, "let the astrologers of the spirit unriddle the portent!"[48]

2

Maksim Gorky: Russian Writer with a Western Bent

Despite the ever-rising flood of essays and monographs on Maksim Gorky discerning readers are still searching for a valid interpretation of the man and the writer and his ambiguous role in the development of Russian letters. The venerable "Father of Soviet literature," the stirring "proletarian writer and humanist," the impassioned "poet of the masses" has been alternately lifted to the stars as a "genius of world literature" and lowered to the limbo of a "minor writer," a "derivative artist imitating the great writers of the past in everything except in their greatness."[1]

Contradictory statements such as these are apt to contribute but little to a fair appreciation of the Russian author. Considering the situation, it will not seem amiss to illuminate some neglected facets of his personality and production—facets pertaining to his attitude toward the literary culture of the West. A scrutiny of this kind may perhaps help counterbalance certain one-sided or biased judgments of Gorky's stature and permit one to view his image in a less-distorted perspective.

It is a historical fact that most Russian writers of the twentieth century adhered to the idealistic radicalism of the

Social Revolutionaries. Very few writers, among them Blok and Gorky, embraced the Marxist type of socialism. Yet paradoxically, Gorky's renowned works are all permeated by the romantic anarchism of the vagabond and the hard-fisted individualism of the merchant: features that do not fit the stereotype image of the "proletarian writer" who thus emerges as a "bourgeois individualist turned inside out."[2] Nonetheless, the apparent paradox can be in part resolved in view of Gorky's youthful enthusiasm for German romantic poetry and for Byron. As may be seen from the memoirs of Vartanyanets, "Gorky in Tiflis," young Maksim was raving about Byron already in 1892: "He [Gorky] frequently called me into his room and with enormous rapture read to me *Manfred* and *Cain.*"[3]

Reminiscent of the pathos of Gorky's romantic models, Byron and Schiller, is likewise his distinct "heroic" tendency. He gave it artistic expression in the metaphor of the bold falcon whose heaven-storming flight challenges the sluggishness of the lowly "earth-bound" creatures.[4] Like Pushkin and other Russian poets, Gorky esteemed in Schiller "not only his artistic genius but above all his concepts of freedom which constitute the substance of his entire activity."[5] In his lyric poetry Schiller uses the metaphor of the eagle to symbolize the lofty aspirations of mankind. The eagle's flight—like the falcon's soaring—represents free and independent thought courageously penetrating the limitless spaces of the unknown. Its "powerful wings" are poetically associated with the image of unrestrained flight into the realm of creative imagination, the realm of happiness and freedom. There is a possibility that even Nietzsche may have contributed to young Gorky's "heroic" temper of mind. Lev Tolstoy at any rate, sensed such an influence and reacted to it sharply: "He [Gorky] unconsciously pays homage to the fashionable ideas of Nietzsche, ideas which I find extremely repugnant."[6]

The parallel Gorky-Ibsen looms large in recent Soviet scholarship. From the Marxist point of view the cardinal problem in the plays of these writers can be reduced to the formula "the individual versus the masses." Of course, such a dialectical statement of the issue already implies its "logical and inevitable solution." Accordingly, it was simply a "sublime fallacy" on the part of Ibsen to assume that the liberation of the individual would necessarily lead to the liberation of the masses. Ibsen causes the enlightened minority to act in opposition to the ignorant majority. The contrary occurs in the dramas of Gorky: the oppressed majority rises against the ruling minority.[7] In *The Wild Duck* and in *Lower Depths,* to be sure, the two playwrights seem to develop their theme in complete solidarity almost to the very end. To Soviet eyes the crucial difference rests on the particular that in Ibsen's play there is "no salvation from ruin and destruction" whereas in *Lower Depths* a "way out of the chaos is opened."[8]

The rationale supporting this ideological juxtaposition of Gorky and Ibsen is uncomplicated, to say the least. Ibsen, the representative of the "decaying middle class," was powerless to extricate himself from the atrocious contradictions of his time and society. Gorky, on the other hand, "solved" almost instinctively the riddle which proved "insoluble to Ibsen." The defects of this kind of reasoning are obvious and the methodology itself is far from original: For it was Belinsky who introduced extra-literary criteria in the evaluation of literary works. But on the basis of such "criteria" Soviet critics undertake to "prove" the superiority of the revolutionary writer opening "a way out of the chaos" over the bourgeois writer whose world ends in "ruin and destruction."

Several points worthy of closer scrutiny can also be derived from a comparison of Gorky and Gerhart Hauptmann. It seems the Russian realized already in his formative years that an artist must have a comprehensive conception of life, and that the problems confronting him were "more complex than the problems encountered by Schiller and Goethe." No wonder, "Gorky, like Hauptmann, immersed himself in the leaden abominations of life in order to study them thoroughly."[9] Gorky's drama *Lower Depths* presumably represents the artistic balance of his "thorough study of life." With reference to Hauptmann it is certainly interesting to note that *Lower Depths* bears much resemblance to *Hanneles Himmelfahrt* in a number of scenes and details.

Gorky's drama begins in a poor-house like the play of Gerhart Hauptmann. There is also a dying girl, Anna, who —comparable to Hannele—emerges as the central figure in the events that follow. Even Luka's consolation to Anna ("Death, let me tell you, is to us like a mother to small children") sounds like an echo of the principal theme in *Hanneles Himmelfahrt.* Nevertheless, a fundamental difference between these two plays must not be passed over in silence: Hannele, in contrast to Anna, does not wish to regain her health. In the finale Hauptmann raises his spectators to the radiant spheres of "Heaven" while Gorky drags them down to the drabness of "earth."

Considering the parallels and differences, can Gorky's *Lower Depths* be interpreted as a reply to Hauptmann's *Hanneles Himmelfahrt?*" Such appears to be the claim although it is conceded that there was "no conscious intention on the part of Gorky to polemize with *Hannele.*"[10] Of course, the plays of the two writers are juxtaposed not merely for the sake of literary analysis. Far more important, from the Soviet perspective again, is the establishment of Gorky's distinct "ideological superiority" over the "opportunistic and reformistic tendencies" of the German dramatist. To that end Gorky's play *Yegor Bulychov* and Hauptmann's *Vor Sonnenuntergang* are adduced as final evidence. Both plays were published in 1932 and both contain—there is no denying—a number of similarities.

Thus, in both works, representatives of the "old world" stand in the center of the events. Both yearn for a new and better life—and both are blocked by the fierce opposition of their relatives. The scene of Hauptmann's play is laid on the eve of the Fascist upheaval while the action of Gorky's play occurs a short time before the outbreak of the Bolshevik revolution. From these generic analogies far-reaching significative and ideological inferences are drawn. The essence of the German drama is seen in terms of a vast socio-political symbolism indicative of the abyss at which mankind has arrived. Gorky's play, on the other hand, is credited with the wizardry of opening before humanity a perspective of "sunrise and liberation."[11] The victory of the "revolutionary principle"—Bulychov sympathizes with the Bolshevik Laptev whereas Klausen yearns for death—inescapably resolves the question of "artistic superiority" and the laurel is given to the singer of "sunrise and life."

In this context it will not seem unapt to recall Gorky's antipathy for suffering and death, his passionate belief that suffering was not an integral and unavoidable ingredient of human existence, but an "abomination" which ought to be swept away from the face of the earth.[12] At a time when Maeterlinck proclaimed the triumph of death over love the author of *The Lower Depths* arose in fervid defense of life, truth, and humanity. Satin's thundering words in the finale constitute perhaps the climax of this defense—simultaneously they are also indicative of the influences and undercurrents that flow through the play. Thus his eulogy of the "man who is strong, who is free," clearly echoes the lyricisms of Nietzsche's superman ethics while his cry, "man lives for something better," resounds with the pathos of Schiller's "Hoffnung": "Zu was Besserm sind wir geboren!" Another theme of the poem ("Noch am Grabe pflanzt er die Hoffnung auf") comes alive in the figure of the pilgrim Luka planting the hope of a transcendent better world in the heart of the dying Anna.[13]

After the failure of the revolution of 1905 Gorky, together with Lunacharsky and others, resolved to counter the widespread disenchantment of the masses by injecting the elixir of religion into the creed of socialism. To be sure, this marriage of Marxism and Christianity was not just another case of "God-seeking" but rather a strange attempt at "God-building" in order to revitalize the faltering revolutionary movement. In this respect Gorky's attitude to religion markedly differs from that of Dostoyevsky, who consumed himself in an anguished struggle to "find" the Creator of this fathomless world. However, one should keep in mind that religious, especially biblical, motifs abound in all of Gorky's works written during those years of frustration. Suffice it to mention his ideological novel *The Mother* (1907) and as a specific example the heroine's well-nigh liturgical ministrations to the revolutionary workers. Even more biblical imagery pervades the novel *A Confession* (1908). It is perhaps here that Gorky gives the most vivid poetic expression to his endeavors to "build God," to create a socialist "religion of the masses." Needless to say, this compromising aspect of his personality and work has not been thrown into relief by Soviet scholarship and thus awaits critical elucidation by reviewers in other parts of the world.[14]

Gorky's exalted notion of the creative genius of the masses must perhaps be viewed in connection with his concept of religion. In terms reminiscent of St. Francis' canticle "The Praises of God's Creatures" ("Sister water who is very useful and humble and precious and chaste"), he invokes the venerable names of Milton and Dante, Mickiewicz, Goethe and Schiller. These writers "rose to their loftiest height precisely when inspired by the creations of the collective, when drawing inspiration from the well of folk poetry which is measurelessly deep, infinitely iridescent, strong and wise."[15] Gorky does not question the right of these poets to everlasting fame but contends that individual genius can provide merely the external form and the luster. Their works may in truth be compared to superbly cut diamonds—yet these diamonds were brought forth by the collective genius of the masses. "Zeus was created by the people. Phidias embodied him in marble."[16]

Gorky felt enthralled by the beauty and power of classical

antiquity but he voiced misgivings about the course of modern civilization. He conceived of nineteenth century literature as a process of gradual decline, a process of corrosion inexorably leading to the "destruction of the individual." Looking upon such luminaries as Goethe, Byron, Schiller, and Shelley he could not help marveling at the spaciousness of their souls, the range of their interests, the depth of their insights and ideas. "Is the spiritual richness of these men not extremely fascinating?" he asked. "But the closer we get to our times the more we observe a melancholy shrinking of concepts and themes, an indigence of feeling and imagination."[17] Reiterating his concept of artistic creativity Gorky accents the point that individual talent alone had not produced up to this time "neither a Prometheus nor a Wilhelm Tell nor a single poetic figure comparable in its shapeliness and vigor to the Hercules of gray antiquity. Manfred is but a degenerated Prometheus of the nineteenth century, an accurately drawn portrait of a burgher-individualist. . . ."[18]

Despite these barbs Gorky held Western literature in the highest esteem and never tired of recommending its study to young aspiring writers who turned to him for help and advice.[19] But at the same time he cautioned them against the dangers of literary serfdom and unimaginative imitation. Conceiving of literary influence in terms of a struggle with the original source he insisted that a young poet seek his own self, discover his authentic voice. Gorky was not satisfied with mere poetic "talent," with its dazzling glitter of "divine sparks." "What we need," he wrote to D.N. Semenovsky, "is a great poet like Pushkin, like Mickiewicz, like Schiller; what we need is a democratic and romantic poet for we, Russia, are a young and democratic country. . . ."[20]

The phrase "democratic and romantic" is very characteristic of Maksim Gorky and might be well used to define his own temperament as a man and writer. Such mental and poetic disposition may also help explain his admiration for certain aspects of West-European literature, which in a large measure harmonized with his socio-political tenets. Thus he gave the highest praise to the "social romanticism of Schiller, Byron, and Hugo," viewing it as "one of the most beautiful creations of the West-European soul, the Sacred Scripture of the genius of real life."[21] And he noted with gratification that "form" was not "the most important thing" to these and other masters of European letters.[22] Gorky's "revolutionary romanticism" provided in the early twenties the Serapion Brothers with a convenient label under which they could devote themselves to the creation of a non-conformist literature relatively free of ideological controls.[23]

Though a revolutionary writer, Gorky often assumed a critical attitude toward the Bolshevik revolution. Like numerous other Russian poets, "he saw few signs of the great moral transformation he had so long awaited."[24] To be sure, there were even fewer signs bespeaking a "great literary transformation," and it was perhaps for this reason that he indefatigably called for the elaboration of a "true critical perspective." Gorky realized that such a perspective could be derived only from a far-ranging evaluation of every kind of literature, including "bourgeois" and "reactionary" literature. Therefore he did not hesitate to encourage his Soviet colleagues—even during the savage years of the civil war—to study the literary heritage of the West exactly for this purpose: "so as to avoid unjustified boasting about what they themselves were producing."[25] It was for the same reason that Gorky established the publishing house "Universal Literature" under the sponsorship of which more than two hundred world classics were made available in excellent translations to the Russian masses. It may seem strange that the initiator of this huge cultural enterprise was not proficient in foreign languages. As a matter of fact, he had to struggle very hard to assimilate the bare linguistic essentials and consequently esteemed the merits of fine translations.[26]

Gorky's autobiographical works and the memoirs of his contemporaries reveal his marked leaning toward Anglo-German romanticism during his crucial formative years. We already mentioned the spell cast on his mind and imagination by the works of Byron and Schiller. At this point one ought to specify that it was principally the German poet who was intensely admired and emulated. Gorky's poem "Mifologema," where love is extolled as the "creator of the world," may serve as an example. It bears a striking resemblance to Schiller's "Phantasie and Laura," with its nearly identical motif: love exalted as the "ruler of the world." Indicative of Gorky's enthusiasm for Schiller is the fact that he loved to recite the poignant monologues of Karl Moor *(Die Räuber)* to his friends. What is more, he even dreamed of playing the role of the "noble-hearted robber" on the stage of a real theater.[27]

In accord with his collectivistic concept of literature, Schiller's drama *Wilhelm Tell* ranked very high in the eyes of the Russian because it issued from the "creative genius of the people." Discoursing on Pushkin's *History of the Revolt of Pugachev,* Gorky compared it to Schiller's *Geschichte des Dreissigjährigen Krieges:* "This is an attempt on the part of the poet [Pushkin] to speak the language of an historian which Schiller spoke in his *Geschichte des Dreissigjährigen Krieges.*"[28]

On another occasion, assessing the various aspects of romanticism, Gorky quoted the German poet as an authority in order to validate his own viewpoint. He sets out by directing attention to the "hundreds and thousands of marvelous poems singing of love." This delicate feeling, he contends, performed the role of a stimulant in arousing the creative powers of mankind. It was through love that man became an infinitely more sociable creature than the most intelligent among the animals. In this evolutionary process the poetry of an earthy, healthy, and active romanticism had an enormous didactic and social impact on the relations between the sexes. " 'Love and hunger rule the world,' said Schiller. At the roots of culture there is love, at the roots of civilization there is hunger."[29]

While propagating an active, life-affirming type of romanticism Gorky simultaneously voiced regret that such a dynamic romanticism was alien to the literature of the Russian nobility. "They were not capable of bringing forth a Schiller and instead of *Robbers* they superbly described *Dead Souls, Living Corpses, Dead Houses, Three Deaths,* and many other deaths. Even *Crime and Punishment* was presumably written by Dostoyevsky to counterbalance Schiller's *The Robbers.*"[30] Needless to say, Gorky was keenly aware of the inroads pessimism had made into the literatures of the West but it was with regret that he acknowledged this fact: "The mood of hopelessness was not unknown to Goethe in his *Faust* nor to Schiller in *Don Carlos* and *Wallenstein.*"[31] Averse to any form of pessimism he valued the "positive and life-affirming" sides in the creations of these and other Western writers. Thus Goethe's "Prometheus" caught his fancy and prompted him to aim for a Russian counterpart, *Vasily Buslayev* (written about 1900), of which, however, only the monologue has been completed. Gorky's image of Prometheus corresponds very closely to the titanic figure in Goethe's poem: he is not just the first rebel revolting against the established order but also the "father of human civilization." This cultural aspect of Promethean insurgency is "placed in the foreground in the monologue of Gorky's Buslayev."[32] Another instance of Goethe's impact on the Russian writer may be seen in the poem "Man" (1903). Of course, despite its kinship with Goethe's *Faust,* this opus cannot be really paralled with Goethe's dramatic masterpiece. But in the limited sphere of artistic motifs and poetic ideas it clearly represents an elaboration and continuation of the problems encountered in Goethe's *Faust.* Specifically, it was Faust's basic optimism, his faith in man and human reason, which greatly endeared him to Gorky. Furthermore, the theme of unflagging "striving," the concept of "work" as one of the supreme values of human existence, the dream of a "free land" ruled by a "free people"—all this aroused a sympathetic echo in the heart of the Russian. Noteworthy, finally, that his important essay "On Plays" (1933) opens under the auspices of the German poet with a citation from *Faust:* "One hundred years ago Goethe declared: 'In the beginning was the deed.' "[33]

It is hardly an exaggeration to contend that Gorky consumed his life with Faustian "deeds" and "dreams." Periods of feverish political activity alternated with romantic dreams of happiness for enslaved mankind. In the sphere of literature he constantly dreamed of the emergence of a "great Russian poet" comparable to the most brilliant writers of the West.[34] For Gorky realized that Russian literature could not boast of a Shakespeare, Calderon, Lope de Vega, Schiller, Kleist, or Hugo: "Nobody can deny, since it is so obvious, that in our country the drama has not reached such heights as in the West." Yet he did not hesitate to give wholehearted praise to the achievements of such Russian playwrights as Griboyedov and Gogol: "Very beautiful our comedies *Woe from Wit* and *Inspector General* . . . by no means inferior to the comedies of Molière and Beaumarchais."[35]

Gorky's remarks about the relationship between art and reality assume an ambiguous ring in Western ears, especially since they come from the initiator and "first classic of Socialist Realism."[36] For a new kind of art is envisioned—nay, postulated—by the dean of Soviet letters which would rise "above reality," which would "elevate man above reality without tearing him away from it." Gorky must have been aware of the ambivalence for he himself raised the question: "Is this the gospel of Romanticism?" The answer is couched in terms of the Soviet "reality" of the 1930s but also in terms of philosophical casuistry: "Yes, indeed—if social heroism, if cultural and revolutionary enthusiasm for the creation of new conditions of life, in those forms in which this enthusiasm manifests itself among us, can be called Romanticism. But, of course, such Romanticism must not be confused with the romanticism of Schiller, Hugo, and the Symbolists."[37]

To all appearance, these remarks reflect an intimate and intricate dilemma in the heart of the Russian writer. On the one hand he demanded a literature that would be Marxist in theory and outlook, on the other hand he desired this literature to develop spontaneously by dint of the sincere convictions of the authors. Gorky evidently did not anticipate that the doctrine of "Socialist Realism" would be exploited by bureaucrats and party zealots to stifle independence of thought and artistic inventiveness. He must have assumed that his enormous prestige would enable him to safeguard a reasonable margin of creative freedom for all Soviet writers—even literary and ideological adversaries who refused to embrace the new dogma. Referring to this troublesome quandary, a critic observes: "It is touching and painful in turn to reread, with the advantage of thirty years hindsight, the writer's [Gorky's] speeches from the First Congress of the Union of Soviet Writers."[38]

Gorky's protracted and intimate affiliation with Stalin reveals a perplexing facet of this author's personality. The question arises how this restless and basically anarchic spirit could become trapped in the snare of despotism. Even more intriguing: By way of what syllogism did he get to the point of extolling some of its most execrable institutions, such as the forced labor camps? There exist no clearcut answers to these baffling questions. But perhaps we will not be too far from the truth if we assume that it was his triumphal return to the Soviet Union (1932), the dizzying blend of glory, fame, and adulation, which blinded him as to the true nature of Stalin's rule. Gorky, the man of letters, was no match for the iron-nerved, coldly calculating politician. As a result, the writer was forced to sanction with his immense renown a literary concept that had the most pernicious consequences for Soviet cultural life. At a certain moment Gorky probably realized the ravages he had wrought on Soviet literature by his theory of "Socialist Realism"—but the damage had been done and reflected, if anything, his increasing impotence in the face of heavy-handed bureaucratic encroachments upon the sphere of art.[39]

Whereas the "proletarian humanist" displayed symptoms of ideological myopia for the iniquities of tyranny in his own country, he promptly and perceptively responded to political danger signals from abroad. Thus the ominous surge of fascism in Germany imbued him with profound apprehensions for the future of European civilization. His essay "On 'Soldierly Ideas' " (1932) mirrors his consternation about the ever-rising tide of barbarism and terrorism:

> To see this delirious madness it was necessary to 'outlive' or 'get rid' of Goethe and Kant, Schiller and Fichte and a hundred of the greatest thinkers, poets, composers, and painters. The treasures of bourgeois culture decay untouched—literally 'untouched'—in libraries and museums, and the life of the bourgeoisie becomes always more filthy and savage, its political rule always more sadistic and inhuman. To be sure, the world beyond the frontiers of the Soviet Union is governed by madmen.[40]

Gorky did not live to witness the climax of this "delirious madness": the devastations and atrocities of the second world war. He passed away in 1936 under suspicious circumstances—allegedly due to a recurrence of his old pulmonary affliction. It would be ironic, indeed, should it be ascertained that his high-minded and gallant "search for an end to the cruelty of Russian life"[41] was cut short by the machination of a ruthless and crafty autocrat with whom he had co-operated for many years. Apparently, contemporary Soviet youth does not rave about the "Father of Socialist Realism" and his literary achievements. But Gorky continues to be very popular with the older generation, to say nothing of the Soviet regime which has apotheosized him as the most illustrious Russian author after Pushkin. The grand official memorial to the patriarch of socialist literature will be a "complete edition" of his works in thirty-three volumes—a landmark in Soviet literary scholarship if printed in strict accord with the centennial announcement.[42]

At this juncture it would seem appropriate to throw into relief Gorky's lifelong preoccupation with Romanticism. Much like Benedetto Croce, he conceived of this movement in terms of a dichotomy: diseased versus wholesome. Thus "passive Romanticism" infected the mind with fear of reality and a desire to escape into a world of abstract dreams. "Active Romanticism," on the other hand, stimulated progressive tendencies arousing the will to change reality and "illuminate the present with the light of the future."[43] Perhaps Gorky was alluding to this "active and progressive Romanticism" when he declared that a Soviet writer should know not only the past and the present but also the "reality of the future," and that this "third reality" ought to be included in his works. In this inclusion of the time to come, in the author's ability to view the present from the vantage point of the future, Gorky recognized "one of the most important characteristics of 'Socialist Realism.' "[44]

To be sure, even Soviet critics do not always agree with Gorky's definitions and evaluations. This is true of his views on the nature of Romanticism and Realism which were upbraided for being "excessively schematic." Also his appraisal of Gogol's role in Russian literary history and his pronouncements on Dostoyevsky have not been well received—ostensibly on account of their "one-sidedness." Yet the critics keep on the safe side by extolling Gorky's acumen at the same time: "It was his merit that he did not separate Realism from Romanticism by a Chinese wall. . . ."[45] As a matter of fact, Gorky embarked on his literary career with a series of stories which represented an intimate fusion of realistic and romantic elements. In the years preceding the first world war he wrote his "Italian Fairy Tales" (1911–13)—another effort to combine stark naturalistic detail with a subdued romantic form. Later, amidst the turmoil and violence of the civil war, he and a few other writers (such as Blok and Lunacharsky) undauntedly rallied to the defense of Romanticism. In the sphere of the drama and, more concretely, in the practice of the revolutionary theater Gorky's attitude contributed to a triumphal revival of the romantic traditions of Schiller and Hugo.[46]

Gorky's penchant for Romanticism was based on his conviction that a new mode of existence could be established only on the solid rock of previous achievements. It was for this very reason that he called on his countrymen to master the cultural heritage of Western civilization, to assimilate "the good, the true, and the beautiful" of the past as an indispensable prerequisite and point of departure for all future victories of the human spirit. To a large extent his noble intentions were thwarted and his message twisted to suit the designs of an intolerant, machine-oriented bureaucracy. Critics of the Russian writer ought to bear in mind that his concept of "Socialist Realism" was not originally devised as an intellectual straitjacket but rather as a general framework with opportunities for foes and friends to create in relative freedom.[47]

Considering Gorky's notions and visions as they are expressed in his works and collating his various critical pronouncements, one may arrive at the conclusion that they constitute a system—a system *sui generis,* to be sure, the component parts of which are not always organically related to one another nor to Marxist ideology. The bulk of his artistic production shows a profusion of chaotic, anarchic, romantic, and pessimistic elements that cannot easily be reconciled with the official optimism he ostensibly displayed. Gorky's entire "philosophy" suffered thus from an irremediable birth flaw which affected in varying degrees the substance of his literary creations: their poetic excellence, the vigor and artistic unity of style. Even so he emerges as a gifted man of letters though not as a "proletarian writer." Most of his plays and novels, except *The Mother,* deal not with the struggle and triumph of the proletariat but rather with the decline of the Russian merchant class. In this respect, Gorky reveals his ties with the cultural tradition of the West and with such authors, among others, as Galsworthy and the brothers Mann, "creators of literary masterpieces and chroniclers of bourgeois decay."[48]

Gorky's renown rose to a high point about the turn of the century. At that time, there developed a widespread feeling that the author of *Lower Depths* had opened a new cycle in European civilization by establishing an original, humanistic literature of the working masses. But the frenzied surge of patriotism during the initial stages of the first world war precipitated a rapid eclipse of his fame. His literary star sank to its nadir in the turbulent years after the Bolshevik revolution when his aesthetic and poetic influence was scarcely felt. Like many other Russian writers, Gorky lost his political ardor and his creative impulse upon confrontation with the realities of Soviet life.[49] He devoted himself to cultural and humanitarian activities and there ensued, as a Marxist critic admits, "a relative stagnation in his artistic productiveness" caused by "ideological reservations and doubts."[50] Gorky's literary renascence in the thirties must be viewed with skepticism: it was a synthetic revival brought about by the Soviet authorities for obvious programmatic reasons. Hence the exaltation of altogether undistinguished works, such as *The Mother* and *Klim Samgin,* which were raised to the rank of "masterpieces of world literature."[51]

Any critic struggling to arrive at a dispassionate appraisal of Maksim Gorky finds himself on the horns of a dilemma. The quandary derives from Gorky's abiding and apparently gratuitous subservience to the aberrations of the Stalinist regime. Despite many attenuating circumstances, the discrepancy between his professed and propagated "socialist humanism" and his eulogistic espousal of the notorious forced labor camps remains hard, if not impossible, to bridge. In consequence, even his most fervid admirers cannot reasonably deny that his credibility as an advocate of the oppressed has been compromised. However, these and similar strictures would not necessarily impair his reputation as a writer since they relate, on the whole, to the peculiarities of his character and the contradictory nature of his oscillating personality. For the sake of fairness a different, that is an aesthetic, criterion ought to be applied to measure the excellence of his literary achievements. Using then an artistic standard of valuation one is obliged to realize that the upheaval of the human condition during the past half century has caused the bulk of Gorky's works to be buried under the ashes of tendentiousness and literary obsolescence.[52]

In contrast to the claims of certain critics, a perceptive reader may fail to discern in Gorky's protagonists those unique and ageless qualities by dint of which they would become "comparable to such figures of world literature as Don Quichote, Till Eulenspiegel, Hamlet, and Faust."[53] As for Gorky's impact on the diversified intellectual and literary evolution of our epoch, it can hardly be termed consequential. Little or no evidence has been produced to corroborate the allegation that his works are "a source of inspiration for the writers of the whole world under the motto of peace, democracy, and humanism."[54]

Nevertheless, after having demolished the image of the "giant of world literature" the Western critic ought to pick up the bricks and raise a life-size, yet still impressive, monument to Maksim Gorky, the author of the unforgettable *Memoirs* and *Literary Portraits.*

3

Blok, Schiller, and the Bolshevik Revolution

Contrary to what might be expected, cultural life did not come to a standstill in Russia during the chaotic years of the revolution and the civil war. A glance at the repertory of the theatres reveals that, at least in this sector, a very intense cultural activity continued despite enormous material difficulties and ideological pressures. Paradoxically, the destroyers of the old society had to turn to the cultural heritage of their enemies to bolster the fighting spirit of the starving masses. And thus we observe a fascinating phenomenon: in Petrograd, the throbbing heart of the revolution, the stage is dominated by the plays of the bourgeois authors Shakespeare and Schiller.

One of the most fervent admirers and popularizers of Schiller in Russia was the poet Aleksandr Blok. It is not always possible to agree with his views regarding the German dramatist, but he did elaborate a number of very striking concepts and evaluations, at any rate concepts characteristic of a certain time or rather frame of mind. On the following pages, Blok's attitude toward Schiller is interpreted as representing a certain style of thought and is therefore seen in historical perspective.

Blok's acquaintance with Schiller's works dates back to the years of his youth. This acquaintance must have been of an intimate nature for in a letter to his mother he affectionately calls him "mein Lehrer Friedrich (v. Schiller)."[1] Many years later, as stage director of the Great Dramatic Theatre in Petersburg, he wrote a number of essays on Shakespeare, Schiller, and other poets—veritable masterpieces of his simple and energetic style—which were read by the actors before the performances to the soldiers of the Red Army. It is in these essays that Blok's attitude toward Schiller comes to light most strikingly.

A few rather interesting ideas were expressed by Blok in his article "The Downfall of Humanism" (1919). He maintains that the crisis of Humanism began during the Reformation with the appearance of the masses and he regards Schiller as the "last great European humanist." Next to Schiller he places the "colossal figure of Goethe" in whom dying Humanism is pervaded with the music of the future—the music of the masses which can be heard in the second part of *Faust.* Marquis Posa *(Don Carlos)* "sings" of mankind for the last time for the style of Humanism, the Baroque, dies together with Schiller.[2] Goethe remains alone—he envisions the future, the tongues of fire which will devour the Baroque temple of enlightened Europe. He joins hands with Richard Wagner, the author of the fire theme in *The Valkyrie,* over the head of Heinrich Heine who is "burning to death" in that very same fire of the future. Though so different from each other, they all are equally lonely and equally persecuted because they are representatives of genuine culture and are heralds of the future. Blok discerns a "secret bond of spiritual affinity even in Goethe's "ambiguous relationship" with Heine and vice versa.

The banner of Humanism intrepidly held high by Schiller was seized by the "tense and eager hands of the people of the nineteenth century." Schiller was the last "tranquil and equilibrated" writer in Europe. After him "we see faces that are disturbed, disfigured, distorted by inner anguish."

Upon rereading Schiller's *Don Carlos,* Blok is struck by the "grandeur of its architecture," by the diversity of conceptions, themes, and ideas" which he incorporated in one single tragedy. The elements of history, art, and music, are all present in this one play—a "modern poet would make ten plays out of this same material." Lost is the balance between man and nature, life and art, science and music, civilization and culture—that "balance by which the great movement of Humanism lived."

It would lead too far to polemize with Blok. However, some of his peremptory statements seem to call for closer examination. This will help to throw into greater relief the difference between his own peculiar point of view and ours —a difference of more than half a century. Thus one might protest that Schiller was not the "last great European humanist" but that after him there came several others: Grillparzer, Benedetto Croce, the brothers Mann, Hermann Hesse, etc. Apart from that, in view of Schiller's early death, one wonders, too, why Goethe is not considered the "last humanist" in Europe. Yet these are relatively minor points. More important seems to be the fact that Schiller is relegated to the "Baroque temple of the past" whereas Goethe —together with Wagner and Heine—is advanced to the rank of "herald of the future." Nothing needs to be said about Heine in this connection, and as for Wagner, there was a time when he fought on the barricades of Dresden together with the anarchist Bakunin (1848).[3] But although the "music of the masses" undoubtedly pervades the finale of the second part of *Faust* ("Solch ein Gewimmel möcht' ich sehn,/Auf freiem Grund mit freiem Volke stehn. . . ."), an important detail can hardly be overlooked: that Goethe's hero actually is little more than a benevolent despot. Moreover, what precisely was Goethe's concept of freedom? "Es ist mit der Freiheit ein wunderlich Ding," he said to Eckermann (January 18, 1827), "und jeder hat leicht genug, wenn er sich nur zu begnügen und zu finden weiss. . . . Hat einer nur so viel Freiheit, um gesund zu leben und sein Gewerbe zu treiben, so hat er genug, und so viel hat leicht ein jeder." Freedom, as Goethe understands it, consists in respecting the God-willed division of society into classes and in fulfilling the duties of one's estate. As far as "freedom" is concerned, Schiller was infinitely more pervaded by the "music of the future" than his conservative friend—proof his *Briefe über die ästhetische Erziehung des Menschen* (1795) which, in a sense, are his impassioned reply to the inhuman excesses of the French revolution.[4]

Blok's attitude toward Goethe and Schiller is revealed in the lines of his essay where he says that if he were a sculptor he never would represent the two poets as shaking hands with one another: "I would model Schiller as a young man leaning forward and dauntlessly gazing into the misty abyss opening in front of him."[5] For Blok this "young man" stands in the shade of the "gigantic and mysterious figure" of Goethe, shrinking back, as it were, before the blinding vision of the future which he beholds in the abyss. Schiller is the lesser figure, but both are equally dear and near to his heart. He loves Goethe because he is not only an end but also a beginning, a "landmark at the frontier of two centuries." And he loves Schiller because he is the "last bard of humanity faithful to the spirit of music." Blok sees the embodiment of this "spirit of music" in the figure of Marquis Posa who "sang of mankind" for the last time. Thereafter mankind was only prosaically discussed from the top of professorial desks and was scrutinized in hundreds of voluminous and respectable books.[6]

There is no denying that Blok had a very peculiar concept of Schiller. Thus it is hard to imagine that the German poet was "surrounded by a music-filled atmosphere of creative tranquillity and leisure." As a matter of fact, Schiller's attitude toward music was lukewarm and nondescript and he certainly was very far from any "tranquillity and leisure." Blok, it appears, chose to ignore Schiller's treatise *Über naive und sentimentalische Dichtung* (1795), in which the German defines himself as a poet of anguish who is longing for the lost unity with nature. Blok's joining together of

Schiller and music brings the former close to the viewpoint of Vyacheslav Ivanov.[7] However, in this specific case, the German romantics and the French symbolists may be cited as possible influences.[8] Blok does not mention Oswald Spengler in his essay but at times one has the impression that the *Untergang des Abendlandes* (1918) was—directly or indirectly—the inspiration for some of the views expressed by the Russian. To single out just one striking parallel: Blok's assertion that the culture of enlightened Europe had died with Schiller corresponds closely to Spengler's cycle theory of cultures according to which the life span of a culture is about one thousand years. Blok's "downfall of Humanism" coincides thus exactly with Spengler's *Untergang des Abendlandes*—both authors regard the year 1800 as the beginning of the decline of Western civilization.[9]

In his capacity of director of the Great Dramatic Theatre in Petrograd, Blok wrote a number of letters to the actress M. F. Andreyeva. We learn that "*Die Räuber* and *Die Jungfrau von Orleans* lie in the air" and that the Petrograd theatre "has already shown its capability of dealing with Schiller."[10] But he added that Shakespeare, Schiller, and similar great tragic writers had to be approached "with uncovered heads." An ostentatious attitude of reverence was necessary in view of the "unbridled and chaotic atmosphere" which prevailed at that time (1919).

Blok—and also his friend, Andrey Bely—had welcomed the revolution of 1917, seeing in it the great storm that was to purge and redeem the Russian people. Now, only two years later, he turned in a mood of intellectual despair to the cultural representatives of the hostile camp because he had found in them the principle of discipline and order which he attempts to uphold against the massive onslaught of laxity and anarchy. A similar attempt of rapprochement with the West may perhaps be seen in his poem *The Scythians,* written in 1918 and containing an impassioned appeal to the Western brethren to unite with the East to evade final disaster.

Shakespeare, "the eternal, the universal-human," is to

Blok the immovable center of the repertoire. After him come Schiller and Hugo followed by Ibsen, Sem Benelli, and Maria Levberg. Sublime romanticism and crass realism, though acting in different directions, each have a place in the revolutionary theatre, as was demonstrated by the triumphal success of Schiller: "For it is impossible not to call the performances of *Don Carlos* a triumph. The fact that the Petersburg public—exhausted and tattered—filled the theatre twenty-six times watching an eighteenth-century tragedy attentively for six long hours, no doubt is almost a miracle." One of the factors which contributed to the victory of *Don Carlos* among the revolutionary masses was the excellence of the actors: "It is a pleasure to know that we have such superior interpreters of Schiller."[11]

Blok's views on the responsibilities of the actors are most interesting. He maintains that—in addition to the things seen and heard on the stage—the spectators take home something intangible, "something of that great world which, as we all feel, is still unexplored and which at times frightens us by its unexploredness: something of the world of art."[12] The representatives of this world of art are authors like Shakespeare and Schiller, but the greatest poets often surpass themselves. "The world of art is greater than any one of us, it is greater than both Schiller and Shakespeare—it is an element of the universe." The vast task and challenge of the actor is this: to give back to the masses part of this blind and elemental world which they themselves have created.

Blok acknowledged the leading role of German romanticism in European literature at the beginning of the nineteenth century. From his analysis of the spirit of romanticism he arrived at several practical conclusions regarding the theatre in general and the revolutionary theatre in Petersburg in particular. Thus he attached great importance to the exalted "Lebensgefühl" to the service and cult of which the romantic theatre had dedicated itself with much fervor. In accord with this, he called for the most expressive, the most sweeping, the most appealing gestures to arouse and electrify the masses. To achieve the desired effect, the actors must be at home in all the periods of history, for in every romantic work there is contained a universal feeling—a feeling, as it were, that is tantamount to a mutual pledge of all mankind. "So, for instance, the grouping representing the friendship of Don Carlos and Marquis Posa is very beautiful and in the highest degree timely when, as it were, in one grand gesture they take the solemn oath to struggle for the welfare of humanity."[13]

Blok's "Discourses" which were read before the performances to the soldiers of the Red Army constitute little masterpieces of his plain and forceful style. Introducing *Don Carlos* by the "great German poet Schiller" to his audiences, he characterized it as a "colossal drama—colossal both in scope and in conception." In contrast to Stankevich and Herzen, who conceived of *Don Carlos* as a tragedy of love, Blok put the principal stress on its political aspect. Accordingly, King Philipp and the "free citizen" Posa were to him the two dominant figures in the drama. However, the author of "Downfall of Humanism" was himself too much of a humanist to overlook the human, personal, individual elements in Schiller's tragedy:

> Great writers do not occupy themselves only with politics; they have to touch upon it perforce but they are occupied with a far more important matter—with art which, together with science, leads to an understanding of the ultimate purpose of life. For this reason great writers are not interested in depicting the kings as gloomy rascals in whom there is nothing human; what interests them in man above all is man as he was created by nature.[14]

Blok alludes here to the figure of King Philipp in Schiller's *Don Carlos* for whose sufferings and sorrows, often hidden behind the paraphernalia of his royal dignity and power, he strives to arouse the sympathy of his audience composed of revolutionary workers and peasants. To many of them it must have been a revelation to realize that unhappiness could dwell also in a heart covered with royal purple and that the powerful ruler of half the world was powerless to free himself from bitter grief.[15]

The Russian poet was aware of the demoralizing influence of power, and perhaps he had contemporary political parallels in mind when he described how the lord of a giant empire surrounded himself with the most loathsome scum of the human race: secret policemen, provocateurs, and spies. But at the same time he pointed out to his listeners that King Philipp was a slave of time and circumstances—a slave of his royal dignity because he could not help killing, could not help signing death sentences, and was neither willing nor able to give up his burdensome power.

Marquis Posa is characterized by Blok as a man free of all conventionalities who did not live for himself and who had only one preoccupation—that all mankind should be happy. "He [Posa] thought, like a child, that it was easy to achieve this. He thought that the King was able to renew the earth with one stroke of the pen."[16] To be sure, there was a moment when the dreams of the Marquis might have become a reality, when the troubled King would have gone out all the way to grant liberties to his suffering subjects. But King Philipp was not alone. Behind him stood the Inquisition—a powerful, cruel, uncontrolled institution which held the opinion that the end justifies the means; an institution which later suffocated from the blood of tens of thousands of its victims. Behind him stood also a brutal and rough soldier, a faithful royal watchdog with a wolfish jaw, the Duke of Alba. And around him there crawled a treacherous horde of spies—creatures that are neither men nor beasts but petty demons. Many abominable things have been thought out by the inhabitants of this beautiful earth. They have invented weapons of destruction and instruments of torture, but certainly they have not devised anything more loathsome than that invisible spiritual torture to which one man subjects another man.

Blok concludes that Schiller's great tragedy terminates with a victory of lie, evil, and death. "What does it teach us? Do we perhaps see not enough lie, evil, and death around us on earth?" The answer to this question was only too obvious in those days of revolutionary upheaval. But Blok derived comfort from the thought that it was not easy, that it was not sweet for the victorious villains to live or even to exist, "that pack of wolves which remained to rule on earth after it had devoured everything good." Their life was not life. It was easier for those cruel and blood-stained gendarmes to choke than to live on earth. Lie and evil carry the seeds of destruction in themselves and "for every evil deed a man will receive his retribution sooner or later."

The "joyful light of good and truth" is then contrasted with the "cheerless gloom of lie and evil." Referring to Posa and Don Carlos in particular, Blok exclaims: "Was the short life of these young men—betrayed and tortured to death by scoundrels—not fuller and happier in every single minute? Note how freely they stride, how their eyes shine, how ardently they speak their minds!"[17] And how disgusting to look at those "creeping reptiles" next to them who do not dare to raise their heads even while they hiss. Life is not a joy to them but "a shame and a torture." Nor can the man who has surrounded himself with such reptiles free himself from heart-rending anguish even though he rules the world.

Such are the lessons the Russian poet derives for himself and his audience from Schiller's "immortal masterpiece." Blok the unswerving humanist reveals himself in no uncertain terms in this analysis of *Don Carlos* which at the same time constitutes a scathing indictment of oppression, terror, and deceit. Considering the historical circumstances, his challenging indictment of "cruel uncontrolled institutions" and "abominable investigations and tortures" might even be construed as a hidden criticism of the revolutionary regime. While it is true that Blok welcomed the "ten days which shook the world" with exuberant enthusaism, it is no less true that his fervor soon abated and that he wrote almost nothing after 1918. The vehemence with which he denounced the shameful practices of the Inquisition may be indicative of the degree of his disillusionment with the course and outcome of the revolution. Blok's analysis of *Don Carlos* shows, however, that he was far from that morbid and hopeless pessimism attributed to him by some critics. "Lie and evil destroy themselves," he told his Red Army soldiers, "for every evil action a man will receive his retribution sooner or later." This certainly does not sound like desperate pessimism but rather like an expression of the belief that good will triumph in the end. In short, it sounds like the teaching of that Christ whom Blok made appear at the head of his twelve Red guardsmen marching on through frost and snow toward a new spring of mankind. Though some critics claim that Blok's use of the Christ symbol remains well-nigh inexplicable, the supposition arises that the poet was hoping for a humanization and Christianization of the Bolshevik revolution.[18] At any rate, what he had fervently dreamed of was a purification and spiritual rebirth of the Russian people but not an abasement into the lower depths of physical and psychological violence. The stark realities of Soviet life overpowered his poetic genius and inspiration, intruded into his innermost self and in the end ruined him from within.

In contrast to the conventional interpretation of *Don Carlos* ("Ideendrama"), Blok sees in it a "didactic" drama that conveys a "moral" and at the same time "pragmatic" lesson: it does not pay to be a villain; lie and evil destroy themselves; even the most powerful mortal cannot escape from suffering and anguish.[19] Blok apparently was fully aware that Schiller's drama went far beyond the narrow limits of didacticism. He confessed that he was "struck" by the "greatness of its architecture," by the "diversity of its conceptions, themes, and ideas." By stating that "the elements of history, art, music, and painting are all present in this one tragedy," he recognized that Schiller's *Don Carlos* was a romantic tragedy *par excellence.* Heroic Posa stands in the center of that romanticism which the more radical-minded Russians called humanism, cosmopolitanism, or democracy. Justly so—for it was Posa who infected even a despot such as King Philipp with the seductive idea of freedom.[20]

In December 1919 Blok wrote a speech on Schiller's *Die Räuber.* The German poet was introduced to the Red Army soldiers as "one of the first fighters for the freedom of Europe and of all mankind."[21] Blok characterized *Die Räuber* as a "prophetic play" which anticipated the great French revolution by eight years. The impassioned speeches of Karl Moor are a "cry of suffering, wrath, and revolutionary revenge hurled in the faces of the tyrants." Blok did not hide his sympathy for the magnanimous robber. Karl Moor is to him a "great heart and a sublime soul" —a revolutionary dreamer who "lives the irreconcilable contradiction between law and freedom." In the name of the welfare of mankind, he asserts his right to break the law and to proclaim freedom because the world is abominable, because people are pitiful and insignificant—creatures without boldness and without backbones, oblivious of mother nature. But Blok rejects the idea that justice on earth can be established by acts of violence and terror: "The ends and motives of Karl Moor were pure but the means through which he acted were unsuitable."

All this seems to imply a belief on the part of the Russian poet that an individual—no matter how noble, honest, incorruptible, and strong-willed—is not able to deal with the evil and injustice prevailing on earth. Common action of the weak and oppressed against the tyrants should therefore be the answer. Karl Moor perished as a robber but "his revolutionary impulse has remained alive."[22] It infected and keeps infecting the minds of people, teaching them to struggle jointly and with arms in their hands. And Blok reminded his audience that only a few years after the "execution" of the noble robber and revolutionary dreamer of

Schiller's play the first great revolution shook France and its neighboring countries.

Blok the theatre director never forgot even for a moment that he had to explain Schiller to rough-hewn workers, peasants, and soldiers. Using strong and simple language adorned with realistic imagery, he strove to arouse his listeners to a realization of the enormous importance of art and literature in the struggle for freedom:

> You do know how many explosives must be put into a cannon so that it can function with force and at a great distance. You also know that with the bare hand, no matter how strongly you swing it, it is quite impossible to deliver such a powerful and hard-hitting stroke as with a cannon—an invention of the human mind.
>
> Now, literature and theatre—creations of the human spirit—have been such cannons to the peoples of Europe in their struggle for freedom; these cannons have been the strongest up to the present time; they act at a far greater distance than any real cannon. Without such cannons the peoples of Europe would not have destroyed so many thrones in the short span of just one hundred and thirty years.[23]

Like his friend Vyacheslav Ivanov, Blok conceived of the poet as an instrument of the gods—a prophet and seer capable of penetrating the mysterious mist of the future. When a thunderstorm gathers in the air, great poets sense the approaching upheaval, although their contemporaries usually do not suspect anything. The soul of the poet, Blok believes, is like a receiver which draws the force of electricity from the air and concentrates its energy in itself. Such was the sensitive soul of the twenty-year-old Schiller. The fire of revolt glowed in his heart, yet he languished in a country divided into hundreds of principalities—amidst a disheartened people who had lost all hope of freedom, under the iron rule of a Duke who was a tyrant. But there was a "thunderstorm" not only in the soul of Schiller. At that time, a tempest and a cataclysm were brewing in the air all over Europe. *Die Räuber* proved a "prophetic play."

Schiller died a premature death. However, his humanistic ideas "have not died with him." The fighters for freedom and human dignity who lived after him became the "eager and rightful heirs" of Schiller's humanism. What is more, his "revolutionary plays" provided a source of comfort and inspiration to the exhausted masses in the difficult period of the civil war:

> The creative spirit of Shakespeare and Schiller was a help to all of us in 1919 because we believed in its absoluteness, in the fact that—it had not died. To be sure, it is not always easy to believe in this in times like ours when the very life of people is torn from top to bottom, when at certain moments it seems that nothing of the old world will remain or has a right to remain.[24]

A noteworthy statement: the spirit of Shakespeare and Schiller had not died on the blood-soaked battlefields of the civil war! In spite of all, a remarkable man like Aleksandr Blok kept believing in such "reactionary chimeras" as the good, the true, the beautiful—and, in addition, he was not alone in his untimely idealism. His belief was shared by good friends and literary allies: Andrey Bely, Vyacheslav Ivanov, and several others. Schiller's thirst for freedom, his unshakable faith in the power of the beautiful were close to the hearts of these mystical symbolists—as close and dear as to Vladimir Solovyov, their venerated teacher.[25] Intrepidly defending the world of the spirit in the whirl of civil war and revolution, Blok predicted an incalculable future of prestige and vitality to the dynamic robber play of the German poet: "Schiller's inspired drama, written one hundred and forty years ago, will not lose its political significance as long as the spirit of struggle is alive in our hearts and as long as the battle-cry resounds: *In tyrannos!*"[26]

In the final analysis, Blok's attitude toward Schiller represents a style of thought, conditioned by personal and historical circumstances, in which the political element overshadows the artistic one. To be sure, this predominance of political considerations was by no means limited to his relationships with a representative of the capitalistic West but extended to some of his greatest and most significant works. Suffice it to mention in this connection his extraordinary poem *The Twelve,* which ultimately may be construed as an attempt on the part of the poet to achieve on the highest possible level a genuine fusion of politics and art. In a sense, the attempt proved a failure both politically and artistically.[27] But could it be otherwise? Wasn't he a Russian Marquis Posa whose exalted dreams were crushed by a new kind of despotism? As a matter of fact, "a wolf and a lamb cannot live side by side—in the end the wolf will devour the lamb. And so it happened."[28] Blok thought of Posa and King Philipp when he wrote these lines which he might have written about himself.

4

A Trailblazer of Russian Westernism: V. P. Botkin

Vasily Petrovich Botkin (1810–69) is known in Russian literature as the author of the brilliant *Letters on Spain* and as an intimate friend of Stankevich, Belinsky, and Granovsky. At Kryazhev's boarding school in Moscow he studied French and German and first acquainted himself with the literature of Western Europe. Unfortunately, instruction was on a woefully inadequate level, and he was hindered rather than stimulated in his intellectual growth. Nevertheless, thanks to his determination and ability, he eventually mastered not only French and German but also English, Italian, and Spanish. A virtual autodidact, without real help or guidance from his uninspiring teachers, Botkin dedicated himself to the acquisition of knowledge and even constructed a carefully meditated philosophy of life. Thus it was exclusively through his own efforts and achievements that he became one of the most remarkable men of his time.

After graduation, Botkin worked as a shop assistant for his father, a tea merchant who showed little discernment regarding the talents of his son. Despite these trammels and the unpropitious atmosphere at home, despite a crowded schedule of exacting, time-consuming business duties, he still found leisure and energy for pursuing his beloved literary and artistic interests: "All his spare time he [Botkin] used for the reading of foreign books. German books prevailed, and so he developed under the influence of German literature which became most important when he joined the famous Stankevich circle."[1] In addition to literature, Botkin was vividly interested in history and natural sciences. Among his artistic interests music and painting held the first place. He intensely loved German music and Beethoven was one of his favorite composers. But he was not satisfied with the passive role of a listener and soon began practicing music himself. He chose the violin as his instrument and he played it with enthusiasm and exquisite skill.

In a letter to the poet Afanasy A. Fet, written in 1862, Botkin recalled—not without melancholy—the onerous years of his childhood and frankly acknowledged his great indebtedness to German literature, thought, and art for the shaping of his taste and the elaboration of his philosophy of life:

> Stankevich, Granovsky—the whole period of my youth draws me toward Germany: for here grew all my best ideals, all my first raptures in music, poetry, and philosophy came from there. . . . I had no real education. After my graduation from the boarding school (a very wretched one) I absolutely had not the slightest notion of anything at all. The world about me was dim as if it were in a mist. From this period I remember only one thing: I read *Fiesco* and *The Robbers* by Schiller and also Zhukovsky's translations from him. It is this experience that for the first time and for ever has established my relationship to Germany.[2]

Thus Botkin was already deeply imbued with the spirit of the German "Storm and Stress," and Schillerean idealism when, after his return to Moscow from a trip to France and Italy (1835–36), he came into closer contact with the Stankevich circle where Schiller and the German idealistic philosophers were the dominant influence. Botkin immediately entered into the spiritual and intellectual interests of the circle and actively participated in its passionate pursuit of knowledge, wisdom, and virtue. His familiarity with foreign languages and literatures gave him at once a great advantage and a position of authority among the other members of the circle: "No wonder then that he [Botkin] was ranked among the first as to volume of literary and aesthetic information."[3]

Surprising as it may seem, there is evidence that Botkin exercised a powerful influence even on the great critic, Belinsky, by directly contributing to the composition of some of his important essays: "No doubt, Botkin sometimes helped Belinsky also with the drafting of his articles. We have the sure testimony of initiated people that the passages on romanticism in these articles do belong to the pen of Botkin."[4] This is an interesting revelation which would seem to modify any claim, on Belinsky's behalf, to originality as a critic of literature.

Botkin's extraordinary qualities were by no means exhausted in his manifold artistic and literary activities where he often remained an amateur, even though a brilliant one. Another important aspect of his personality may be seen in his profound and utterly sincere humaneness. He was a generous and benevolent friend to all who knew him. This was especially true in the case of Belinsky, with whom Botkin shared not only his ideas but quite often also his better-filled purse.

All his life Botkin was an avid and insatiable reader. Hand in hand with his boundless thirst of knowledge went a jealous fear of overlooking something interesting or important within the rising flood of publications. Thus it was a matter of course that even after the loss of sight on his left eye he did not pass a single day without serious reading. In June 1863, a few years before his death, he remarked one day to Fet: "The history of India is my gap and I must needs fill it." Then he showed his brother-in-law (Fet was married to Botkin's sister Marya Petrovna) many voluminous tomes of extremely fine print. Fet was startled: "Good gracious," I thought, "this man stands at the edge of his grave and with his one remaining eye—through glasses—he still tries to fill out gaps. Amazing!"[5]

The year 1838 brought an abrupt reversion in Botkin's aesthetic and philosophical views. Parallel to his now cooler attitude toward Schiller went an increasing enthusiasm for realism and reality brought about by the teachings of his friend Bakunin. After Stankevich's departure from Russia (1837), Bakunin, a formidable debater, became the unchallenged authority on German philosophy in the circle. It was Bakunin who first proclaimed his unconditional "reconciliation with reality" in an article printed in the periodical *Moskovsky Nabludatel* (1838). Bakunin's impassioned speeches glorifying the doctrine of the old, conservative Hegel produced an iconoclastic ferment among the members of the circle. Botkin too became infected by the outbreak of the anti-idealistic fever and soon succumbed under the irresistible onslaught of Bakunin's soul-stirring eloquence. Together with Bakunin and Belinsky, "Botkin participated in denouncing idealism and glorifying reality."[6]

Shortly after Belinsky's departure for St. Petersburg (1839), the Stankevich circle disintegrated. Botkin gradually lost his enthusiasm for Bakunin's "glorious Russian reality" and for realism in general, and in 1842 he ruefully returned to his former romantic idealism and to Schiller. In accordance with his spiritual renascence, human dignity and the inalienable rights of the individual again became high and sacred ideals to Botkin. This was also the year when Botkin openly associated himself with the Westerners by joining the circles of Granovsky, Herzen, and Ogarev. In a letter of March 22, 1842, in a mood that anticipates the revolutionary events of the year 1848, Botkin quotes a verse from Schiller's *Wilhelm Tell* that must have seemed to him, as it were, the epitome of the aspirations and hopes of his progressive-minded generation:

Das Alte stürzt, es ändert sich die Zeit
Und neues Leben blüht aus den Ruinen.

It may be significant that, in the same letter, there are also references to David Friedrich Strauss, Ludwig Feuerbach, and Bruno Bauer. Although his reborn romanticism prevented him from accepting their positivistic views at that time, he nonetheless showed the keenest interest in the development and in all manifestations of German philosophic thought.

Thus, when Herzen returned from his exile to Moscow in 1840, Botkin, along with others, recognized him as one of the city's leading intellectuals. Two years later, the Russian intellectuals were sharply split into Westerners and Slavophiles. Herzen made common cause with the champions of a Western-oriented liberalism. Botkin followed his example and before long became one of the most militant standard-bearers of the Westerners. As a contributor to the periodicals *Otechestvennye Zapiski* and *Sovremennik* he kept the Russian public informed about the cultural life flourishing beyond the frontiers.

Proof of his vigorous activity in the sphere of criticism can be found in his travel reports, his musical analyses, his sketches on romanticism, his essays on Carlyle, Dante, and Shakespeare ("Botkin was an avowed lover of Shakespeare and one of his best connoisseurs"[7]), and in his articles on German literature. There is subtlety and keen perception in his writings. He emerges as a critic who penetrates artistic and literary phenomena and appraises them on the basis of a well-rounded aesthetic and philosophical system. Last but not least, his works reveal him as a writer of unusual quality—a writer "who holds the gift of brilliant and distinct representation and of captivating story-telling."[8]

In his searching review of German literature, Botkin depicted a panorama of German cultural life about 1843. At the outset, he described and analyzed the discord and sharp struggle of two German philosophical schools: the followers of Hegel and the followers of Schelling. L. Jagemann's *Reisenotizen* inspired him to attempt a survey of new currents in German painting, the plays of Hans Koester—to discuss the state of contemporary German drama. In connection with the publication of a German version of the works of Dickens, Botkin considered and evaluated the German attitude toward the English writer. Reviewing several anthologies of German lyric poetry, he took the occasion to reflect on the contemporary concepts of love while Gutzkow's *Letters from Paris* caused him to turn to pictures of French political and cultural life. Finally, there were Weiske's monograph on *The Myths of Prometheus* and Wüstermann's learned essay *On the Use of the Rose among the Ancients* which "gave him [Botkin] an opportunity to plunge into the sweet epicurism of ancient life."[9]

Botkin's zeal in acquainting the Russian public with the latest developments on the Western cultural scene often brought him into bitter conflicts with the censor. Seeing an abundance of fascinating Western books on the market, he was more than eager to bring them to the attention of his countrymen. Unfortunately, in many cases he found that he could not do so because of the fears and rigors of the Russian bureaucracy. In a letter of May 20, 1843, written to his publisher Krayevsky, he acrimoniously complained about the enormous difficulties of reviewing certain foreign books in a Russian periodical:

> German literature now presents this peculiarity that if spirited books of this kind are published they are all imbued with such a tendency that discussing them in a magazine becomes an impossibility. The whole current literature of polemics between Hegelianism and Schellingianism belongs to such a category, for in the centre of this quarrel stand religion and Christianity.[10]

Botkin was infuriated by this impossibility of reporting on new foreign books which he considered interesting and important, but, since there was nothing he could do to modify this state of affairs, he eventually became discouraged and developed a sense of disgust and frustration.

Botkin's reviews of German literature not only offer examples of his keen observation and his insight into the workings of the German mind but they also throw light on his attitude toward Schiller. Commenting on the tragedies by Hans Koester *(Maria Stuart, Luisa Amidei, Paolo and Francesca, Konradin),* Botkin indulgently remarks: "Koester reveals a great talent—and although it is clear that he imitates Shakespeare yet such imitation does him honor."[11] Turning to the German theatre in general, Botkin arrives at the conclusion that it was living in a vacuum: detached from real life, devoid of great ideas and soul-stirring passions, out of touch with the moving and clashing forces of the time. Among the German playwrights only Schiller could be exempted from this reproach:

> Only one German poet wrote tragedies of a higher contemporary significance. But even he wrote them rather as a result of a general German historical consciousness than from direct, sincere participation in the events that were taking their course. . . . It costs a German poet always a great effort to create a connection between his play and his audience, to inspire them with a profound compassion for the enacted scenes. Schiller . . . particularly succeeded in this respect because his very time, so replete with fear, hopes, and great passions, made the public unusually receptive to the impressions of art. After Schiller, however, they have written for the stage without enthusiasm, without passion, without having first fortified themselves by great contemplations and great ideas. The boredom preying on German domestic life pervaded also the dramatic performances: tragedy did not strive to shake the soul, to arouse the fury of wrath, the fervor of love—in one word, to embrace directly and courageously eternal truth. The works of the great German master, born from his ardent craving for a new order of society, were banned from the stage or else the author was forced to sever relations with the contemporary world. The theatre was bound to go into decline.[12]

There is much truth and critical acumen in the remarks of the Russian although he seems to ignore the existence of such significant and original dramatists as Kleist, Grillparzer, Grabbe, Büchner, and Hebbel. If he had known them he would have found it difficult to criticize the German theatre after Schiller for lack of enthusiasm, raging passions, and great ideas. Botkin probably was thinking of Iffland, Kotzebue, and their imitators—playwrights who stood highest in popular esteem not only in Germany but also in Russia and, as a matter of fact, throughout Europe.

In his review of German poetry, Botkin examined works by Bernhard Reil, Georg Schirges, and Eginhard (Gotthard Freiherr von Buschmann). Considering the significance and validity of their achievements, he arrived at the conclusion that "for our time such poetry is belated and inadequate."[13] What Botkin particularly disliked in these authors —and in German contemporary poetry in general—was their pathological concept of romantic love:

> Schiller inimitably brings out all the excentric morbidness of romantic love in his "Ritter Toggenburg." Also his Ritter Delorges ("Der Handschuh") flinging his glove in the face of his lady represents a pungent and noble protest against a romanticism which has come to a dead end. This in turn derives from the fact that both in its tenets and in its practice there has been so little real consummation of family life and matrimonial love.[14]

Botkin then cites Rückert, "the most prominent of the described love poets," who "personifies the utter decline of this lyric genre more strikingly than anyone else."[15] It appears that Botkin's low esteem of Rückert has been borne out by literary criticism.[16] His wholesale condemnation of contemporary German poetry, however, seems hardly justified in the light of such prominent names as Chamisso, Lenau, Mörike, Droste-Hülshoff, and Platen. Once more, as in his strong denunciation of the German theatre, the limitations of Botkin's literary appraisals become apparent. Perhaps his verdict would have been different if more source material had been available to him at the time when he was writing his reviews.

The year 1843 proved disastrous for Botkin in more than one respect. The crisis was brought about by a beautiful French adventuress whom he married in open defiance of his dismayed family. They were no sooner aboard the ship bound for France, than a violent quarrel arose between the newlyweds. Upon arrival in Le Havre the breach had become irremediable and Armance abandoned her husband. Botkin fell into a state of depression and "all of a sudden lost all his paraphernalia of an extreme idealist" (P. V. Annenkov). He became skeptical, even cynical, and recklessly abandoned himself to a life of uninhibited debauchery. His philosophy of life, his optimism collapsed like a house of cards under the impact of this unhappy affair (a vivid account of which was given by Alexander Herzen in his *Byloye i dumy*). After this terrible blow Botkin did not return to Russia but proceeded directly to Paris.

Botkin was still in the French capital in the fall of 1844 when the Shakespeare translator N.M. Satin, a member of the Herzen circle, arrived from Berlin. His glowing reports about German intellectual life rekindled Botkin's enthusiasm for German culture. In a letter to Ogarev (February 17, 1845), Botkin voiced deep satisfaction with the ferment stirring throughout Germany:

> Germany does not sleep! No, philosophy has not passed in vain through Germany! Of course, theoretical boldness is not yet practical boldness. But important is the fact that Germany has been reared in theoretical boldness. This must inevitably lead to practical boldness—especially when the Germans will reach the conclusion that philosophy is not an end in itself, and that an isolated philosophizing individual is not yet the World Spirit in the act of embodiment; and further that its purpose is not to make the individual free (and what significance has a freedom that is abstract and confined to the soul?).—But not this is important at the present time. Once more the eternal problem is raised in all its implacable severity. Man is abandoning the kingdom of fantasies and entering his arduous philosophical stage in which he must conquer his kingdom of reality and his dignity.[17]

Botkin did not mention any names but we may assume that he was alluding to the ferment introduced into philosophy by the writings of the radical followers of Hegel (Strauss, Feuerbach, Ruge, Bauer, Marx). His reference to the "kingdom of reality" would seem to indicate that he had altogether renounced his former romantic philosophy of life in favor of a positivistic and social-revolutionary attitude.

In 1845, Botkin made his long-prepared trip beyond the Pyrenees which bore fruit in his excellent *Letters on Spain.* In Russia where little or nothing was known of that country before Botkin, his *Letters on Spain* became a great literary sensation. Among his travel books these Spanish impressions probably rank highest as to interest, originality, and brilliance of style, and he owed to them most of his fame among the reading public. Indeed, this renown was not confined to Russia but extended into Western Europe where his *Letters on Spain* were received as a remarkable novelty and "even included in foreign (especially German) bibliographies."[18]

After his return to Russia in November 1846, Botkin again began writing articles on German, English, and Russian literature. Noteworthy among these essays is his critical appraisal of Fet (1856), written on the occasion of the publication of the poetic works of the latter. One of its reflective passages deals with the powerful influence of art upon the human mind:

> There are works of art the echo of which lingers in the soul of the reader for many years and even for a whole lifetime. The work itself and its content have been forgotten long since—but its melody has mysteriously merged with the universal life of our soul, it has fused with our spiritual organism, it has become our sacred and unconscious sentiment which manifests itself throughout our life. Anyone who read Schiller in his youth will presumably agree with us in this matter. Speaking in general: whatever has once appeared in the world does never disappear without a trace—and this earthly, transitory existence of man is destined for a limitless series of echoes.[19]

Botkin's final remarks are reminiscent of Goethe's *Faust*:

> Es kann die Spur von meinen Erdetagen
> Nicht in Aeonen untergehn!—

The rest of the quotation seems to imply that Botkin never ceased to live under the secret spell of Schiller's poetry, and that in fact it had become an integral part of his spiritual existence.

Already in the following year (1857) the urge to travel became again so intense in Botkin that he abandoned everything and left for France. He returned to Russia in 1858 but not for long. Within a year he was on the move once more, went to England and stayed in London for about two weeks. Allowing for some exaggeration, one may say that sicknesses and journeys constituted the chief components of Botkin's life during his last twelve years:

> The restless spirit of traveling . . . dragged him [Botkin] through all these years from one end of Europe to the other, to health resorts, cultural centres, historical places—but peace of mind he did not find anywhere. Then, for brief intervals, he returned to Russia, yet in his home land he felt unneeded and superfluous.[20]

Botkin's only consolation during these years of suffering and frustration was the fullest possible enjoyment of beauty in all its manifestations. The new generation declared war on romanticism and idealism, they rejected and derided that "Schöngeistigkeit" ("fair-souledness") which to Botkin represented both the sense of life and the foundation of his artistic and literary activity. True, the romantic idealism of his youth had well-nigh collapsed. "But although Botkin had in earnest renounced romanticism long since he was, nonetheless, a romantic by his *Weltgefühl.*"[21] As the years went by, his ardent interest in literature and philosophy began to wane and toward the end of his life music—especially the music of Beethoven—became the dominant element.

In 1862, Botkin took another trip to Germany. He passed through Berlin in August and here, on German soil dear to his heart, memories of bygone days overwhelmed him with particular force: Stankevich, Granovsky—the whole period of his youthful enthusiasm for German idealistic philosophy and for Schiller rose again vividly before his eyes. Nearly in a state of rapture, he roamed through the streets of the Prussian capital, frequented the theatres, and enjoyed the works of German literature in the lavish setting of efficiently played stage performances. Sharp-minded and philosophically inclined as he was, Botkin could not help reflecting on the significant differences between Germany and Russia. In a letter to Fet (August 28, 1862), he first described his mood of satisfaction and joy brought about by his arrival in Berlin:

> Clear, warm weather and my strength restored after two days of rest. Finally a feeling of sincere delight which always pervades me when I step on German soil. All this fills my heart with a perfect happiness which I crave to share with you, dear friends. In Berlin I feel at home although I know it very little.[22]

Then, commenting on the prosperous state of German agriculture and comparing it with the conditions prevailing in the Russian countryside, he sadly and wistfully exclaimed:

> Dear friend, all the time I had you and your Stepanovka [Fet's estate] before my eyes. How well this [Germany's] poor soil is worked, how much manure is put on these meagre fields! What would the Germans do with the soil of Stepanovka! When you come from muddy Poland into the German land you pass, as it were, into some kind of brighter country. Poor Slavs! We are scandalized at Gogol for ranking the Germans higher than the Slavs—alas! everyone can convince himself with his own eyes.[23]

After this excursion into the sphere of agriculture, Botkin returns to his reflections on Berlin interspersing them with considerations of a more general nature about the national spirit of the two countries:

> Yes, *es wird mir behaglich zu Muthe* here. This comes chiefly from the fact that all my spiritual development is connected with Germany. I don't even speak of philosophy and poetry—also the German humor is to my liking. Alas! Our so-called Russian education directs us more toward French morals and manners, and this is a pity! . . . The German spirit, which is all discipline, does not tally with our nature. Too bad the Russian travelers pass through Berlin without even trying to grasp it! Only good schools can save us from this kind of superficiality.[24]

Recalling his enthusiasm for Schiller and the significant role the German poet had played in shaping his conception of life and in determining his relationship toward the West, recalling also his friendship with Stankevich and Granovsky who had initiated him into German philosophy and the works of Schiller, he then continues in a mood of melancholy and resignation:

> And so—in my declining years—I greet again this country which first awakened in my soul all that is dear to it until now. When all is done and said, how little does a man change! They say old age is a return to childhood. No, not to childhood but rather to youth! The more I ponder over myself, the more I find in myself that which I was in my youth. Strange, even my ideals have not changed in the least—except that resignation and suffering have been added.[25]

To Botkin's own words may be joined the testimony of his friend and brother-in-law Fet that "certain aspects of German romanticism—especially a contemplative soulfulness *(Gemüth)*—did survive in Botkin's character."[26]

The remainder of the letter contains, among other things, a lively description of his daily promenades through one of the famous parks of Berlin: "Every morning I take a leisurely walk in the shady alleys of the *Tiergarten.* It is marvelously comforting—and everything is so beautiful. . . . May God grant you the same sensation of inexplicable happiness and inner harmony which at present fills my soul."[27] Carried away by his memories and his romantic attachment to the land of Goethe and Schiller, Botkin even indulged in reveries of acquiring a peaceful chalet somewhere in

Germany so that he would have a place of refuge for the time when his doctors would advise him to leave Russia for ever.

Botkin returned to his native country in 1863 but not for long. In the following year, his spirit of restlessness got the better of his Russian patriotism and he departed for Germany and Italy. When passing through Warsaw, the center of a massive Polish uprising against Russia (1863–65), he saw and heard things which were too much for his sensitive, aesthetic nature. He became physically ill and had to stay in bed for seven days before being able to continue his journey. After his recovery, Botkin moved to Venice, where he devoted himself with zeal and passion to the enjoyment of art and the study of the "very noble Renaissance style." In 1865 we find him again in Germany and in Berlin. He remained there for about two weeks and, of course, "did not miss the opportunity to attend various interesting lectures by university professors frequenting even two lectures a day."[28]

During the last few years of his life, Botkin resigned himself to the role of a "superfluous man" seeking consolation in the most refined enjoyment of art. His days and nights were filled with music. He maintained a private orchestra in his palace in St. Petersburg to have music at his command whenever he felt inclined to abandon himself to its magic. One night, after the performance of three Beethoven quartets, Botkin exclaimed: "This was far more than a pleasure—this was a voluptuous ecstasy and, like all voluptuousness, it ends in exhaustion."[29] In a letter of November 27, 1867, Botkin gave an answer to the question what role was still left to him in life: "I value art for the rapture it gives to me—and for all the rest I do not care."[30] Thus, after years of inner struggles and torments, he finally set his mind at rest.

Botkin passed the year 1869 traveling in the south and west. He stayed on the island of Ischia for some time but in the fall he moved to Aachen in the hope of finding relief for his crippling paralysis by bathing in the warm mineral springs that abound near that city. However, his condition deteriorated steadily and he had to be treated by his brother Sergey Petrovich, a renowned physician. For all that, his spirit remained unbroken and he even conceived the idea of writing a comprehensive *History of Art.* Fate did not permit him to carry out his ambitious plan.

Toward the end of his days he suffered from an acute feeling of loss and frustration. A short time before his death he complained to his friends: "My life has been a failure—I should have become a professor."[31] On October 10, 1869, Botkin—writer, critic, journalist, aesthete, admirer of Western culture—quietly passed away in his sumptuous palace at St. Petersburg. Death came as a redeemer to him delivering him from the tortures of a chair-bound but not at all "superfluous" existence. In his will Botkin bequeathed a substantial part of his fortune to various cultural institutions for the advancement of art and science and for the assistance of needy students.

Soviet criticism has tended to minimize Botkin's importance for quite obvious ideological reasons. The main charges are "underestimation of Russian culture" and "admiration for the bourgeois culture of Western Europe."[32] Other charges are leveled at his snobism, aestheticism, and the desertion of his liberal ideals: "In the sixties he [Botkin] openly passed into the camp of reaction proclaiming the idealistic theory of 'art for art's sake' and attacking the democratic-revolutionary views of *Sovremennik* and Herzen's *Kolokol.*" The ostracism extends even to Botkin's articles on music (1830–50) in which Beethoven, Chopin, Mozart, and the popular-realistic elements of Italian opera feature as models against superficial virtuosity, scholastic prejudices, and learned routine: "The basic fault of Botkin's musical criticism lay in the fact that he ignored the greatest phenomena of Russian national music of that time—the works of Glinka and A.S. Dargomyshsky."[33]

It is significant that Botkin's brother Sergey Petrovich,

the "founder of the physiological approach in clinical medicine," has received official Soviet recognition (one of the greatest hospitals in Moscow was named after him), whereas Vasily Petrovich, the "worshiper of Western bourgeois culture," has been committed to well-nigh complete oblivion. Botkin's works—published at St. Petersburg in 1890—have not been reprinted since the revolution. In the twenties some credit was given to his *Letters on Spain* and his essays on Fet, Ogarev, and Shakespeare. His correspondence was described as "extremely important" for the history of Westernism in Russia: "As a matter of fact, it is through Botkin's letters that one can establish the special role Botkin played among the 'Westerners.' "[34] Yet even such limited recognition was conceded grudgingly and very little has been done up to the present to define and evaluate Botkin's "special role" in the circles of Stankevich, Belinsky, and Herzen.

To ignore the achievement of V. P. Botkin is virtually to belittle or deny the importance of Western thought in Russian culture. A recognition of Botkin's contribution rights a balance in Russian studies which has for too long been tipped toward the East.

5

T. N. Granovsky and the Ideological Lure of the West

Almost as legendary as Stankevich and as fascinating a phenomenon in the history of Russian intellectual life, T.N. Granovsky (1813–55) attracted much attention as a splendid lecturer, polished writer, and idol of Russian youth in the early forties. A young man himself—he was only twenty-six when he was appointed professor of history at the University of Moscow —he inspired his students to undertake a fundamental review and reevaluation of the issues which Western Europe, and particularly Germany, presented to Russia. As one of the standard-bearers of the Westerners, he saw the answer to the woes and problems of Russia in a decisive reorientation of Russian society in the direction of the ideals of German humanism. In his lectures and writings he indefatigably "called Russia to the disciplining influence of law, culture, and free political institutions."[1]

Granovsky was born in Orel on the Oka river. After graduating from Kister's Boarding School in Moscow, he went in 1831 to St. Petersburg and obtained a position in the Ministry of Foreign Affairs, where Count Strogonov became his friend and protector. Officially, Granovsky studied law at the University, but privately he devoted most of his time to history, philosophy, and literature. "At this time, literature played a great role in the ideological development of Granovsky. It was with enthusiasm that he read Pushkin, Shakespeare, Schiller, and the historical novels of Walter Scott, which had been his favorite reading even in childhood."[2]

Granovsky's adherence to the German-oriented Stankevich circle (1832–35) fanned his desire to visit the countries of the West and to drink from the very fountains of Western knowledge. To be sure, his means did not permit him to hope for a realization of this dream, but luckily, soon after the completion of his courses at the University, Count Strogonov obtained for him a government scholarship which enabled him to continue his education abroad. Granovsky chose Berlin as his place of study, a characteristic and revealing choice indicative of his interest in German culture and his craving to "plunge into the 'German Sea' of that time so that his humane sentiments might be recast into an integral and solid ideological system."[3] He arrived in Berlin in the spring of 1836 and immediately enrolled in courses given by the foremost German scholars—Ranke, Ritter, Raumer, Savigny, and Werder.

During his stay abroad, the most diverse influences combined to bear upon Granovsky's receptive and sympathetic nature. An important influence was the theatre and in particular the tragedies of Schiller, whose dynamic aestheticism helped him overcome moments of despair and dejection, and whose *Don Carlos* gave him new faith in mankind and life. A soul-shaking experience was his acquaintance with D. F. Strauss's *Das Leben Jesu,* which frightened him by the destructiveness of its ideas. From Schiller and Strauss he turned to the study of the classical languages, to history, geography, and law. In a letter of July 25, 1836, Granovsky told his friend Yanuary M. Neverov about his experiences in the Prussian capital:

> I think I already wrote you on the score of the good opera here, but better than anything else in Berlin is tragedy. I saw *Kabale und Liebe* and *Wallenstein's Tod,* and I cannot describe to you the impression which the simple, in the fullest sense of the word, unaffected, and natural acting of the German actors has made upon me. About Mme. Krelinger I need not tell you anything; you have of course heard a lot about her. She is already getting on in years but is still magnificent, and in the role of Lady Milford she was so charming that Ferdinand's refusal appeared incomprehensible to me. Her two daughters were trained by her for the theatre: the older one—Bertha Stich, a seventeen-year-old girl—is as lovely as an angel and resembles her mother in her acting. She is made for the dramas of Schiller. A real Thekla. I am not very extravagant with tears, but I cried like a little child.[4]

It seems a little surprising that Granovsky, the hard-working and conscientious student of history, did not feel any urge to comment on the figure of Wallenstein or on Schiller's *Geschichte des Dreissigjährigen Krieges,* although the recipient of the letter, Neverov, was a most enthusiastic admirer of the German poet. Instead, he enlarged upon the merits of Mme. Krelinger and the charms of her daughters. The reason for this may have been his serious moral ailment, "le mauvais génie," as he himself called it, and which periodically took complete possession of his soul. These fits of despondency were due to his lack of faith in his own forces and his recurrent consuming doubts about the possibility of reaching the heights of his exalted aspirations.

For a long time neither the exhortations nor the efforts of his friends were able to cure him of his hypochondria. It was only after he had seen the actress Krelinger in the dramas of Schiller that his confidence and good spirits returned. Probably for this important psychological reason he emphasized so much the achievements of the actors and passed over in silence the historical background of the plays. Moreover, at that time he looked at a performance not with the scrutinizing eye of an historian but rapturously abandoned himself to its romantic aspects of poetic beauty, soul-shaking pathos, and redeeming catharsis. This becomes clear from a letter of October 1836, which Granovsky wrote to his sister Varvara:

> Le spectacle est devenu pour moi un véritable besoin: il y a des pièces qui me font vraiment du bien; après les avoir vues je reviens chez moi plus heureux, meilleur et plus capable de travailler. Les drames de Schiller surtout produisent en moi cet effet![5]

Toward the end of the year, the sublimating and revivifying impact of Schiller's tragedies upon Granovsky's "mauvais génie" increased in amplitude and intensity. In a fit of spleen and dejection (because of the prolonged silence of his sisters), Granovsky confided to his friend Neverov:

> What should I tell you about myself?—I work, I read the German poets, and I frequent the theatres three times a week. We had a performance of *Wallensteins Lager* here recently. You certainly know the music written by Weber for the choruses in this divine Prologue, and you know by heart the choruses themselves. As far as I am concerned—I know them by rote. Never yet has art acted upon my soul so powerfully as on this occasion. The combination of magnificent music with the sublimest poetry to which Schiller has risen has produced such an impression on my soul that I will not forget it until death. One of these days they are going to give *Götz von Berlichingen.* Really, sometimes I am completely happy in the theatre. I forget the petty things of this despicable life. I become better and believe in the possibility of characters like Posa.[6]

Bravo for Granovsky's critical acumen and literary taste! Not many Germans in 1836 would have assigned to *Wallenstein* as high a rank as the Russian does when he speaks of the "sublimest poetry to which Schiller has risen." Granovsky's last remarks suggest some familiarity with Schiller's philosophical and aesthetic writings. His moral "betterment" resulting from the salutary influence of the theatre points in the direction of Schiller's conception of the theatre as a "moralische Bildungsanstalt" and of the *Briefe über die ästhetische Erziehung des Menschen.* Less critical perspicacity is shown by Granovsky in his overestimation of Marquis Posa, that presumed paragon of self-denying nobleness. Elated with the poetic grandeur of Schiller's tragedy, he failed to perceive the cryptic ambiguity in Posa's dealings with Don Carlos and the King.[7]

During his stay abroad, Granovsky lived most of the time in Berlin, taking only one trip to Dresden and another one to Vienna. Little is known about his visit to Dresden, but when in Vienna he seized the occasion to attend several performances at the renowned *Wiener Burgtheater.* In a letter to Stankevich and Neverov (dated May 26, 1838), he exclaims in excited anticipation: "Tomorrow I shall see him (the Austrian actor Anschütz) in the role of Wilhelm Tell. Just imagine this drama being given here!"[8]

Granovsky greatly marveled at the liberalism of the Austrian government. How could a play be performed on the stage of the Imperial Theatre in which Austrian despotism was indicted and—far worse—in which the assassination of an Austrian governor was glorified? No doubt, Granovsky thought of the crass rigors of censorship in his native country where even the reading of Schiller's play was construed by the authorities as an incriminating act, nay as "proof of the existence of a conspiracy . . . to assassinate the Tsar."[9]

Soon, on June 12, 1838, he dispatched another letter to Stankevich and Neverov criticizing the plays he had meanwhile seen at the *Burgtheater* and evaluating the performance of the actors: "*Gemma di Vergi,* by Donizetti (rot!). Not long ago Schiller's *W. Tell* was given (how do you like that?) and *Macbeth.* Anschütz played the principal role in both dramas and was really magnificent."[10] As may be inferred from the reference to *Wilhelm Tell,* Granovsky had not yet managed to overcome his amazement at the fact that this poignant drama could be performed publicly in the very country which in the piece plays the role of the villain.

In the same message to Stankevich and Neverov we find

an extended and noteworthy passage which shows how utterly smitten with German literature he was at that stage of his intellectual growth:

> At present I am reading (during the night) Schiller's correspondence with Goethe. Yesterday, I became engrossed in my reading until two o'clock in the morning—I could not tear myself away. How many new things! In their ten years of friendship neither of them published anything without previously showing it to the other and revising it according to the other's advice. The second volume contains Schiller's comments on *Meister,* which truly are a boon to the soul. For heaven's sake, do read these six volumes (little ones); you will become better men, to be sure. Schiller was well aware of Goethe's genius and he proclaims this fact openly. Goethe, on the other hand, called Schiller his prophet: "He makes me conscious of that which I have grasped by poetic instinct."—"Sie erklären mir meine eigenen Träume." They both had no particular esteem for J. Paul. What I read before in Spazier is therefore partially true. They were quite prankish fellows: they liked to crack jokes at their friends' expense. Schiller especially was very fond of such things, and in journalistic controversy he did not distinguish himself by excessive meekness. It is really amusing to read his naive threats. The whole affair with the "Xenien" (epigrams directed against a great part of the contemporary German writers), comes here to light. It is remarkable that only Schiller was held responsible for all such escapades: they were ascribed to him alone—and Goethe was left in peace as if he were innocent. All of Goethe's works written during this period (from 1794 to 1804) are here analyzed by Schiller. There are many very beautiful thoughts on art and on poetry. It is a long time, indeed, since I have read a book with so much profit and enjoyment. Again it occurred to me that one of these days I ought to tackle the literary history of Weimar from Goethe's arrival there until his death. But at the present time I am mature enough only for the biography, the external-historical aspect of such a work, the rest—at this moment—is "dark water in the clouds." From the correspondence between Schiller and Goethe many good things could be selected for our public. Which one of you would like to review the book?[11]

Granovsky's letter proves interesting and illuminating in several respects. First, it shows that the correspondence between the two poets was a revelation to Granovsky who suddenly began to discern new and unexpected dimensions in their personalities. For a long time, Schiller had been to him above all the soul-stirring dramatist, the author of the entrancing *Don Carlos* and the overpowering *Wallenstein.* But now the image of a richer and more complex character arose out of the poet's correspondence with Goethe. Behind the solemn façade of the tragic playwright, Granovsky suddenly perceived the countenance of a man whose features appeared to say: *Nihil humani a me alienum puto.* He discovered Schiller's unexpected thoroughly human aspects—the touching, amusing, and downright funny sides of his everyday existence. He took notice of his penchant for genuine friendship and marveled at the intimacy and magnanimity of his relationship with the older and more famous Goethe. His new awareness of Schiller's critical and satirical talents stimulated his excitement to such a degree that he could hardly wait until his friends in Russia too would participate in his joyful exaltation: "For heaven's sake, do read these six volumes!" But literature had for Granovsky a moral and didactic function, therefore, immediately following, the characteristic sequel: ". . . you will become better men."

Then comes Granovsky's casual but telling remark about the small esteem in which Jean Paul was held by the two German master poets: "Consequently, what I read before in Spazier is partially true." Granovsky, it appears, did not accept the authority of Spazier, but he bowed to the authority of Goethe and Schiller: *Roma locuta, causa finita*—and Jean Paul could be relegated to a lower rank in his esteem without hesitation and further thought. Certainly an interesting example of the sway the German poets held over the mind of the Russian.

Of equal interest is Granovsky's apt reference to the "Xenien" as "journalistic controversy." Here again, Granovsky showed himself to be a reader of discernment and perception. By using this expression, he appropriately rated and classified the "Xenien," anticipating the verdict of contemporary literary criticism. And finally the symptomatic reaction: "It is a long time since I have read a book with so much profit and enjoyment." A characteristic trait of the Russian admirer of Goethe and Schiller comes to light: he is not satisfied to have "so much profit and enjoyment" by himself alone but at once craves to share with others. He thinks of his friends and the Russian reading public and how much they would benefit from a translation of this extraordinary correspondence. In all fairness, credit must be given to Granovsky for having recognized already, in 1838, the value of this epistolary dialogue between two of Europe's most original and inexhaustible minds.

In the fall of 1839, after the completion of his studies, Granovsky returned to his homeland where he received the chair of World History at the University of Moscow. His fascinating lectures attracted huge crowds of students and his fame soon outshone all other Russian professors. Despite his many new duties, Granovsky did not cease to be interested in German literature—proof being his literary feud with Belinsky who at that time embraced "reality" as his "god" and "idol":

> Belinsky's tendency often caused conflicts between him and Granovsky in the sphere of literary opinions. Schiller especially was the object of heated arguments between them. . . . Belinsky began to see the essence of life in reality and the essence of art in objectivity. The idealistic poetry of Schiller, so he believed at that time, was deceitful both in life and art. With all the fury of his new infatuation, he started hating Schiller "for his subjective and moral viewpoint and for his terrible idea of duty. . . ."[12]

Granovsky stood up as a staunch defender of the German poet, but the heated debates between him and Belinsky failed to change the conviction of either one. It is noteworthy that no vacillations or ideological somersaults disturbed the continuity of Granovsky's philosophical beliefs

—in contrast to Belinsky and Bakunin, whose sudden hostility to "subjective poetry" and "deceitful idealism" resulted in a rejection of a whole period of their own work and life. Nothing of the sort occurred in Granovsky's life: "The lofty and idealistic aspirations of his youth—love of mankind and sublime moral concepts which he derived from the grand poetry of Schiller—remained forever dear to Granovsky's heart."[13]

A letter of October 1839, addressed to Stankevich, is indicative of his indignation at Belinsky's sweeping repudiation of idealism:

> He [Belinsky] despises me for my lack of artistic excellence, for my esteem of Schiller, and Uhland, and others. Katkov (a man of high talents) has fallen in with these ideas. On the whole, philosophy has done much harm to them. You would not believe the things they say and write: "*Wallenstein* a pitiful, insignificant work—declamation without life." *Boris Godunov,* on the other hand, "equal to everything written by Shakespeare, not at all worse than *Othello* or *Romeo.*"[14]

It was the philosophy of the old conservative Hegel which had done "much harm" both to Belinsky and to many other members of the Stankevich circle. Under its impact they arrived at a rejection of aestheticism and a reactionary "reconciliation with reality," particularly with "glorious Russian reality." Granovsky's indignation at the disparagement of *Wallenstein* becomes understandable in view of the high esteem in which he held that "sublimest poetry to which Schiller had risen." At that time, Granovsky and Botkin stood almost alone in their defense of Schillerean idealism, but it was comforting for them to know that their ideas would find an echo in the soul of their like-minded, though faraway, friend Stankevich.

Granovsky's circle in Moscow was teeming with intellectual activities throughout the winter of 1839–40. A vivid account of the various events may be found in another letter to Stankevich (written February 12–24, 1840), which also shows that Granovsky's literary feud with Belinsky had not abated in the least:

> We are having many meetings. Redkin [a Moscow university professor], whom I have drawn into our circle, organized regular readings on Saturdays. Actually, we wanted to work on logic together—but the whole thing is not in operation. I simply cannot stand organized meetings for the purpose of studying. My soul loves freedom! Instead of this, we now read Schiller together with Mishel [Bakunin]. Belinsky is now on the warpath in Petersburg. Everybody gets a wigging. Sometimes it is amusing to read him but sometimes also annoying. Moreover, he begins to repeat himself. He keeps silence about Schiller whom he once—in print!—placed on a level with Zagoskin. He must have realized that he has pulled a boner.[15]

Granovsky did not specify which particular work of Schiller he was reading together with Bakunin, but his "My soul loves freedom" offers a very good clue. It is very much like Karl Moor's exclamation in the tavern at the Saxonian border: "Mein Atem dürstet nach Freiheit!" Noteworthy also is the reference to Bakunin, "he shares our views," a comment which seems to imply that Bakunin, the originator and eloquent champion of the cult of objectivity, had in the meantime abandoned his position of "reconciliation with reality" while Belinsky, his exalted pupil, continued waging a quixotic war on idealism under the banner of Hegel.

Granovsky derived so much pleasure and spiritual uplift from his study of Schiller that at times he worked with almost missionary zeal to propagate the writings of the German poet. Thus, for instance, he encouraged his cousin Anna Yevgenevna Kromida to read attentively a biography of Schiller, and her request for his opinion elicited the following reply:

> Quant à la biographie de Schiller par Schwab, c'est un livre fait sans pretention, mais qui se lit bien. La vie d'un homme qui était plus qu'un grand poète, qui a été le héros et defenseur de tous les grands intérêts de l'humanité, mérite d'être connue même dans ses particularités.[16]

Noteworthy here is the stressing of the social and humanitarian aspects—Schiller the "heroic champion of the best aspirations of mankind"—which define the German poet for Granovsky, as it were, for the first time. Until now, Schiller had been to him the author of admirable verse which pacified and revivified his ailing soul. His earlier pronouncements on the author of *Don Carlos* and *Wallenstein* supply abundant evidence in this respect. As for Anna Yevgenevna, she apparently took her cousin's words to heart. Within a year Granovsky deemed her sufficiently steeped in the details of Schiller's biography and the intricacies of the German language to grapple with the works themselves: "Voulez-vous que je vous envoie Schiller? Je puis vous envoyer l'original et une bonne traduction française qui vous en facilitera la lecture."[17]

It seems strange at first glance that Schiller's historical writings are all but ignored by the Russian professor of universal history. The reason may perhaps be seen in the fact that history, as a science, had enormously progressed since the time Schiller wrote his superb but unacademic historical treatises (1787–92). Granovsky, the student of Ranke, was bound to consider Schiller's historical scholarship as obsolete, inadequate, and superseded—superseded by the "objective" and "critical" approach of the founder of modern historiography.[18] Besides Ranke, it was especially his study of Hegel which contributed considerably to the molding of Granovsky's conception of history and to his tendency to regard history as a process in which a line of progressive development could be discerned. Granovsky considered the moral and enlightened personality, immune from the designs of destiny, and a society corresponding to the aspirations of such a personality as the ultimate goal of the historical process. It is this concept which constitutes the very core of Granovsky's philosophy of history.[19]

To be sure, at this point one cannot help seeing the parallel to Schiller's inaugural lecture, "Was heisst und zu welchem Ende studiert man Universalgeschichte?" (1789), where the poet, addressing his students, declared:

> Es ist keiner unter Ihnen allen, dem Geschichte nicht etwas Wichtiges zu sagen hätte; alle noch so verschiedenen Bahnen Ihrer künftigen Bestimmung verknüpfen sich irgendwo mit derselben; aber e i n e Bestimmung teilen Sie alle auf gleiche Weise miteinander, diejenige, welche Sie auf die Welt mitbrachten—sich als Menschen auszubilden—und zu dem Menschen eben redet die Geschichte.

Apparently, Granovsky's concept of the "moral and enlightened personality" substantially coincides with Schiller's postulate of "growth of human personality" in which the attributes "moral" and "enlightened" are not expressed but, in effect, implied.

In addition to this general correspondence of ideas, a more specific instance of Schiller's influence on the historical views of the Russian can be brought forward. We are referring to Granovsky's lecture "On the Contemporary Condition and Significance of Universal History," delivered at the University of Moscow on January 12, 1852. In a crucial passage of his discourse, Granovsky made the following telling remarks:

> Even in its present very imperfect form, universal history—more than any other science—develops in us a true sense of reality and that nobel tolerance without which there is no real comprehension of man. It reveals the difference existing between the eternal, absolute foundation of morals and the limited understanding of these foundations in a given period of time. Only with such a yardstick ought the deeds of past generations to be measured. Schiller once said that death is the great reconciler. These words may be applied to our science. It adduces for every historical misdeed also the circumstances extenuating the guilt of the offender, whoever he may be—a whole nation or a single person. Please permit me to say that he is not an historian who is unable to transplant into the past a lively sentiment of love for his fellow man and to recognize a brother in a stranger separated from him by centuries.[20]

The whole passage and particularly Granovsky's distinction between "absolute" and "conventional" morality vividly suggest Schiller's train of thought in his "Universalgeschichte":

> Sie [universal history] wird Ihren Geist von der gemeinen und kleinlichen Ansicht moralischer Dinge entwöhnen, und, indem sie vor Ihren Augen das grosse Gemälde der Zeiten und Völker auseinanderbreitet, wird sie die vorschnellen Entscheidungen des Augenblicks und die beschränkten Urteile der Selbstsucht verbessern. Indem sie den Menschen gewöhnt, sich mit der ganzen Vergangenheit zusammenzufassen und mit seinen Schlüssen in die ferne Zukunft vorauszueilen: so verbirgt sie die Grenzen von Geburt und Tod, die das Leben des Menschen so eng und so drückend umschliessen, so breitet sie optisch täuschend sein kurzes Dasein in einen unendlichen Raum aus, und führt das Individuum unvermerkt in die Gattung hinüber.

Here we face, indeed, the archetype of Granovsky's "true sense of reality" and "that noble tolerance without which there is no real comprehension of man."[21] The analogy with the argument in Schiller's "Universalgeschichte" is carried further, however, by Granovsky's insistence that historical events must be seen and judged in their proper perspective by taking account of the motives and the accompanying circumstances. The comparable passage in Schiller's "Universalgeschichte" advances this point in the following terms:

> Wie regellos auch die Freiheit des Menschen mit dem Weltlauf zu schalten scheine, ruhig sieht sie [history] dem verworrenen Spiele zu: denn ihr weitreichender Blick entdeckt schon von ferne, wo diese regellos schweifende Freiheit am Bande der Notwendigkeit geleitet wird. Was sie dem strafenden Gewissen eines Gregors und Cromwells geheim hält, eilt sie der Menschheit zu offenbaren: dass der selbstsüchtige Mensch niedrige Zwecke zwar verfolgen kann, aber unbewusst vortreffliche befördert.[22]

Death was the "great reconciler of mankind" also to the Russian. Surveying the development of the human race with the impartial eye of the historian, Granovsky discerned mitigating and even expiatory elements in the most shameful periods of history, and in the heart of the most wicked malefactor he detected redeeming impulses which had remained hidden from the short-sighted tribunal of the contemporaries.

Granovsky preserved a singular sensitivity to literary phenomena throughout his life. Pushkin attracted him more powerfully than any other Russian writer. Among the coryphées of Western letters he singled out Schiller, Goethe, and Emerson for the lion's share of his affection.[23] By temperament an orator, he wrote reluctantly and without enthusiasm. For this reason, there was no possibility of his leaving to posterity as much as he gave to his contemporaries. It was chiefly through his popular appeal, through the magnetism of his personality and his great forensic talent that his renown was spread in Moscow and all over Russia.

Granovsky's declining years were overshadowed by severe fits of melancholy and apathy. To make things worse, these were the years when the tide of political and intellectual reaction was ominously rising throughout the continent. Depressed, Granovsky began to gamble, an activity which did not improve his agitated frame of mind. But to literature and poetry he remained faithful to the last: "Time and again he [Granovsky] commented on his cherished verses from Goethe and Schiller, reciting them by heart or reaching for a book to read them aloud in a circle of friends.[24] "He died," wrote Herzen, "surrounded by the love of the new generation, by the sympathy of all educated Russians."[25]

What about the place and significance of Granovsky in post-revolutionary Russia? Doubtless, there has been a remarkable revival of interest in the historical theories of the "eminent Russian scholar and social activist"—proof being the above-mentioned works by S. A. Asinovskaya and, more recently, N. V. Minayeva.[26] Although he was never able to "rise to the revolutionary democratism of Herzen and Belinsky, who were his close friends," nonetheless credit is given to him for having "masterly utilized the material of Western medieval history in order to denounce the regime of Nikolay in Russia."[27] Numerous quotations from the works of radical writers such as Herzen and Chernyshevsky can be cited to highlight the "liberalism" and "progressiveness" of Granovsky's philosophy of history. Accordingly, Soviet institutional criticism accords high praise to Granovsky's polemic with M. P. Pogodin and M. M. Stasyulevich, both staunch defenders of the "reactionary concept of 'pure science.'" Granovsky, on the other hand, maintained that it was one of the principal tasks of the science of history to "serve the interests of social progress."

However, when all is said and done, even the Marxist critics are forced to admit that Granovsky remained an idealist to the end of his life. True, he turned away from Hegel in the years of his maturity, but only to embrace another form of idealism, viz., positivism. He conceived of history in terms of the natural sciences and emphasized the necessity of studying the influence of the geographical environment on the development of society—a concept reminiscent of the "milieu theory" of Hippolyte Taine. Special attention was given by Granovsky to the periods of transition in history: the fall of the Roman empire, the struggle of the communes for independence, the English revolution of the seventeenth century, and particularly the great French revolution of the eighteenth century, denoting the transition from feudalism to capitalism.

From the Soviet point of view, Granovsky's critique of the "chauvinistic conceptions" of German historiography (Möser, Eichhorn, Grimm, etc.) represents an especially praiseworthy achievement: "He [Granovsky] has shown that the ancient Teutons were not the only ones who destroyed the Roman Empire, but that there was a second destructive force—the mass movement of the peoples of the Roman Empire itself. . . ."[28] Exception is also taken to the "reactionary bourgeois view" that the social level of the Germanic tribes was close to the level of the Romans. In the eyes of Soviet historiography this concept constitutes "a step back in comparison with the theories of Granovsky."

On the other hand, regret is voiced by Soviet historians that his idealistic views prevented him from understanding the very essence and nature of the state (according to Granovsky, the result of the development of the juridical conceptions of the people). Furthermore, he is charged with overestimating the historical role of the monarchic state and the church—a "misconception" which continued to flourish in the theories of the so-called "state historical school" (S. M. Solovyov, K. D. Kavelin, and B. N. Chicherin). In conclusion, however, tribute is paid to him for his "great contributions" to the development of Russian Byzantine and Slavic studies, notably for his emphasis on the "tremendous importance of the Slavs in the fortunes of Byzantium."[29] As a matter of fact, Granovsky's imaginative thesis proved enthralling to several Russian historians such as the byzantinists V. G. Vasilyevsky and F. I. Uspensky, who elaborated upon it and made it an integral part of their historical conceptions.

Up to now, Western scholars have shown little interest in this fascinating figure who stands at the borderline between history, literature, and philosophy. But Granovsky—the champion of Anglo-German literature and constitutional government—belongs both to the West and the East. A Western biography of Granovsky and a translation of his works would serve the double purpose of acquainting Western readers with a remarkable representative of Russian intellectual life and of widening the horizon of Soviet scholarship, which perforce functions within the narrow limits of a rigidly defined ideology. In the last analysis, even a scholarly controversy might prove more beneficial and fruitful than the grandest solitary monologue.

6

Pushkin's Third Dimension: The German Influence

Evidence is now available which sheds light on the phenomenon of Schiller's spectacular prestige in Russia from 1782 to the present.[1] But while it is agreed that "almost all great Russian poets and thinkers passed through a 'Schillerean' period,"[2] the opinion still prevails that Pushkin gave a wide berth to the acclaimed author of *The Robbers.*[3] Strangely enough, it was the Schiller enthusiast Dostoyevsky who first advanced the idea of Pushkin's remoteness from the German poet. In an impulsive letter to his brother Mikhail, dated January 1, 1840, he emphatically declared: "I have never paralleled Pushkin with Schiller.... There is not the slightest resemblance between the two."[4] Half a century later, an analogous view was propounded by a literary historian: "Pushkin did not read German and, due to the peculiarities of his nature, did not fully sympathize with Schiller."[5]

The time-honored notion of Pushkin's indifference toward Schiller and other German poets has survived three revolutions and two world wars. Indeed, it has become almost an axiom in Soviet Pushkin scholarship. Most critics appear to have acquiesced in the presumption of Pushkin's orginality and uniqueness—the distinctive uniqueness of a thoroughly "Russian" poet who owes little to the literatures of foreign nations. As a result, "comparative studies on Puškin have, for all practical purposes, ceased to appear in the Soviet Union."[6]

Of course, this is not a wholesome situation. The time has perhaps come to shed light on a creative relationship that has rested in obscurity for too long. The following pages challenge a preconception and a myth which are divorced from the realities of Pushkin's life.[7]

It is a fact that Pushkin was initiated into the German language in early childhood. One of his governesses, a certain Mrs. Lorsch, gave him regular lessons but apparently with only modest success, judging from the results of his entrance examinations for the Lyceum. Aleksandr attained good marks in French and Russian, yet his knowledge of German grammar was found to be less than satisfactory. Pushkin's report card for the academic year 1812 did not show an improvement: "German Literature: no progress—has no flair for it. Does not apply himself and has no interest in it. Ruined by his previous education."[8]

But only two years later Pushkin wrote his poem "Romance" which reveals clear traces of Schiller's influence both in content and form. Surprising, indeed. Whence this sudden interest in German literature for which he allegedly had "no flair"? No clear-cut answer can be given to this question. However, it would seem plausible to assume that Pushkin was inspired by M. V. Milonov's translation of a poem by Schiller published in *Vestnik Yevropy* in 1813. Refracted in the prism of his poetic soul, this translation may have prompted him to sympathetic musings on the theme of illicit love.[9] Milonov, in the wake of Schiller's "Die Kindsmörderin" (1782), had voiced his indignation at faithless lovers profiting by the inexperience of an innocent maiden, thus driving her onto the road of despair and delinquency.

Undeniably, Pushkin's version departs in certain suggestive particulars from the Milonov-Schiller model. Thus "Die Kindsmörderin" articulates relatively little of that concern for innocent human suffering which reverberates from the lines of "Romance." Ill-starred Luise seems to be an example of feminine weakness and melodramatic rapture rather than a victim of social injustice. The musings of Pushkin's Laura, on the other hand, amount to an indictment leveled not at an individual but at society in general, principally at its prejudices and inequitable laws which discriminate against "children of love" and their unfortunate mothers. The treacherous paramour is ignored—there are neither reproaches nor complaints about his faithlessness. In conclusion, the mother does not kill her child, but she refuses to accept social ostracism. Not having the strength to struggle with human prejudices, she abandons the infant at the threshold of a lonely hut.[10]

Much controversy has been provoked by Pushkin's drinking song "Punshevaya pesnya" (1816), apparently a rendering of Schiller's sparkling "Punschlied" and—oddly enough—the only German poem he ever considered worthy of this distinction.[11] P. V. Annenkov and after him G. N. Gennady and G. D. Vladimirsky expressed serious doubts regarding Pushkin's authorship of this verse, Annenkov without giving any reasons at all and Gennady advancing the hypothesis that it was actually written by Pushkin's brother Lev.[12] Other critics, however, do not see a solid basis for such unsubstantiated suspicions. They contend—and with weightier arguments—that despite Pushkin's indifferent knowledge of German the translation of "Punschlied" can still be ascribed to him: first and foremost because of the conspicuous absence of linguistic difficulties in the original, and in the second place because the task could easily be accomplished with the help of a schoolmate who was proficient in German, such as Wilhelm Küchelbecker, the later Decembrist poet, with whom Pushkin carried on many a conversation about "Schiller, and glory, and love" ("October 19, 1825"). Regarding the merits of the rendition, it was characterized by Leonid Maykov as "very close though not very successful."[13]

Intimately connected with Schiller's "Punschlied" is also the poem "Zazdravny kubok" ("Toast Cup," 1816). Yet the critic Belinsky hailed "Zazdravny kubok" as one of those works by Pushkin in which "the typically Pushkinian poetic element can already be discerned behind the imitation."[14] Evidently, Belinsky had no knowledge of "Punshevaya pesnya" and its interesting relationship to "Zazdravny kubok." It was precisely with reference to this close connection between the two poems that V. P. Gayevsky remarked:

> The philosophy and phraseology of the great German poet, to which Pushkin as a translator submitted in this specific case ["Punschlied"], also inspired him to write his drinking song "Zazdravny kubok." Clearly, there cannot be the shadow of a doubt that it is pervaded by Schiller's spirit and poetic meter. Of course, this poem does not rank among his best, but its youthful freshness and the spontaneity of its Bacchic exuberance appealed to a great master of sounds, Glinka, who magnificently set it to music. . . . Afterwards, "Zazdravny kubok" was adopted by the Moscow gypsies.[15]

In the house of Engelhardt, the Director of the Lyceum at Tsarskoye Selo, Pushkin was introduced to a beautiful young lady, Mary Smith, née Charon la Rose, who had recently lost her husband. Spirited and amiable, she at once caught the fancy of Pushkin, who sent her a rather inappropriate poem entitled "K molodoy vdove" ("To a Young Widow," 1816). In essence, it amounted to a refutation of the romantic idea of "faithfulness beyond the grave" and an unceremonious invitation to bestow her affection upon the author of the verse. The young widow took offense. She had "not only not forgotten her husband but was even then with child by him."[16]

As for the origin of Pushkin's inspiration, it is not difficult to see that he elaborated the theme of Zhukovsky's "Torzhestvo pobediteley," the Russian version of Schiller's notable poem "Das Siegesfest":

Let the dead repose in peace!
Who survives must relish living![17]

Through the good offices of Milonov and Zhukovsky, the German poet left a distinct imprint on various other pieces of young Pushkin. It appears that the philosophical poem "Das Ideal und das Leben" was of particular importance to him at that time, for its principal motifs found a sympathetic echo in such verses as "Epistle to Prince A. M. Gorchakov" (1816), "To A. A. Shishkov" (1816), "I'm yours again, oh my beloved friends" (1816), and several others.[18]

In a humorous note to Zhukovsky written in 1817, which nonetheless may be indicative of his literary interests and serious readings, Pushkin conveyed his "regards to Goethe, Gray, Thompson [sic], and Schiller." Then, tongue in cheek, he slyly added: "I have the honor to convey my regards to them but I'm truly heartbroken that I can never find them at home."[19]

Pushkin graduated from the Lyceum at Tsarskoye Selo on June 9, 1817. His diploma features excellent attainments in Russian, Latin, and French but shows no specific marks in German and German Rhetoric, although both subjects were taught at the Lyceum. There is only the laconic and unilluminating statement: "Furthermore, he has studied History, Geography, Statistics, Mathematics, and German."[20] However, such terseness might be indicative of the fact that Pushkin had not made much progress in his study of German during his six years at the Lyceum and that, as in 1812, he apparently still had "no flair for it." At this point it will not seem amiss to stress one important particular: Pushkin's presumptive lack of "flair" for the *German language* did by no means, as we have already seen, extend to *German literature*.

Following his graduation from the Lyceum, during the turbulent years of his life as an official in the Foreign Ministry at St. Petersburg, "Pushkin became a full-fledged theatre habitué, 'an honorary citizen of the backstage, a severe theatre critic, and an inconstant admirer of lovely actresses.' "[21] It was especially the talented actress Yekaterina Semyonova, with whom he eventually struck up a personal acquaintance, who immediately occupied a prominent place in his theatrical experiences. During the period from 1817 to 1820, Pushkin frequently had the opportunity of admiring Semyonova in her favorite roles. She acted with equal skill in Russian and non-Russian tragedies, including plays by Voltaire, Shakespeare, and Schiller. In these circumstances, it does not appear unlikely that he saw her in Sheller's stage adaptation of Schiller's *Maria Stuart* on December 11, 1817.[22] Pushkin, like most of his contemporaries, held the histrionic accomplishments of Semyonova in the highest esteem: "As far as Russian tragedy is concerned," he declared in his *Notes on the Russian Theatre* (1820), "one must speak of Semyonova and, perhaps, of her alone."[23]

In the days of his exile in Southern Russia, Pushkin composed a short romantic poem, "The Robber Brothers" (1821), the title of which is reminiscent of Schiller's drama *The Robbers.* Another parallel to Schiller may be seen in the cryptic political allusions that so greatly appealed to Prince Pyotr A. Vyazemsky and other Russian liberals.[24] In those restless years before the Decembrist revolution sociopolitical questions loomed large on the intellectual horizon. Opposition to unbridled autocracy was widespread among the educated classes, and a "political" interpretation of "The Robber Brothers" suggested itself readily. To be sure, Pushkin himself had probably not intended to arm his poem with political barbs. His robber is not a noble-minded romantic hero like the robbers of Nodier or Schiller. What is more, Pushkin does not extenuate or exonerate the misdeeds of the brigands, nor does he intimate in any way admiration for their crimes. Nevertheless, contemporary Russian critics took cognizance of the fact that he somehow contrived to arouse the sympathy of the readers for the lawless protagonist of his poem. Thus a certain dubiousness and perplexity insinuated themselves into the minds of the public as to the real significance and interpretation of "The Robber Brothers."[25] Maybe it was due to this subtle ambivalence that Belinsky could not bring himself to relish the poem: "Everything in it is false, everything is strained, everything is melodramatic . . . this poem is an inscrutable thing. Its robbers look very much like Schiller's third-class braves of the gang of Karl Moor, though one can see from the circumstances of the occurrence that it could happen only in Russia."[26]

An awareness of the German poet and his works accompanied Pushkin throughout his stay in the unloved South. Thus we deduce from the draft of a letter to N. I. Gnedich (written in Kishinev on April 29, 1822), that he was acquainted even with episodical details of Schiller's verses: "Fascinating the myth of Pygmalion embracing the cold marble, it engaged the glowing imagination of Rousseau [and Schiller]. . . ."[27] In point of fact, Pygmalion is mentioned by Schiller—though not prominently—in his poems "Der Triumph der Liebe" (1781) and "Die Ideale" (1795). It may seem noteworthy that a few years later the figure of Pygmalion turns up in Pushkin's masterful *Yevgeny Onegin* (IV, 2). Perhaps it was the memory of Rousseau's and Schiller's fascination with the ancient Greek legend which inspired him to allude to Pygmalion in his own work.

In the Fall of 1822 word reached the exiled poet that Schiller's play *Die Jungfrau von Orleans,* in the translation by Zhukovsky, was scheduled for its first performance on the stage of the St. Petersburg theatre. This was exciting literary news, and Pushkin became both thrilled and worried about the prospects of success or failure. From Kishinev he wrote to his brother Lev Sergeyevich:

> With trepidation I hope for a victory of *The [Maid of] Orleans.* But the actors, the actors! Unrhymed pentameters demand an entirely new way of declamation. Being a thousand miles away I can hear the dramatic-triumphant roar of Glukhorev. The

play will be performed in the style of Rolla's death [Kotzebue, *Die Spanier in Peru* (1802)]. What will the magnificent Semyonova do with such a wretched cast? Lord help us and have mercy—but I am terrified. Do not forget to apprise me of this event and ask Zhukovsky for a ticket for the first night on behalf of me.[28]

It was in Odessa that Pushkin turned to a serious study of French Classicist tragedy. Approximately at the same time (1823) he became an avid and enthusiastic reader of Goethe, Dante, Schiller, Shakespeare, the brothers Schlegel, and Walter Scott. In a diary entry he specified those qualities in the great English and German poets which, in his eyes, raised them far above the French Classicist playwrights:

> Sch[iller], Goethe, W[alter] S [cott] do not display a servile preference for Kings and Heroes—They don't bear a resemblance (like the heroes of French tragedies) to servants imitating *la dignité* et *la noblesse*—Ils sont familiers dans les circonstances ordinaires de la vie, leur parole n'a rien d'affecté, de théâtral même dans les circonstances solennelles—car les grandes circonstances leur sont familières.[29]

Considering Pushkin's high esteem for these English and German authors, it does not appear surprising that their works were the very first he insistently demanded from his brother Lev Sergeyevich while planning and elaborating his own poetic production. In a letter from Mikhaylovskoye, the place of his second exile, he specifies: "Send me Fouché, *Oeuvres dramatiques de Schiller,* Schlegel, *Don Juan,* Scott, Goethe. . . ."[30] To be sure, Pushkin had another good reason to be so insistent with his brother. Obviously, the dramatic works of Schiller were badly needed by him for the same reason as the works of Sismondi and Schlegel, namely "for the then seething work on *Boris Godunov.*"[31] Nicholas Rayevsky may have been an additional influence, for he urged Pushkin to consult for his *Boris Godunov* the historical sources used by Karamzin instead of only relying on what *Karamzin himself* had written: "Don't forget that Schiller took a course in astrology before embarking on his *Wallenstein.*"[32]

It is from Schiller that Pushkin learned the "best rules for a tragedy": "the inevitability of the situations and the naturalness of the dialogue."[33] There can be little doubt that he learned his lesson well and that he took advantage of Schiller's two dramatic principles in his *Boris Godunov.* As for the substance of the play, its indebtedness to Racine must be thrown into relief while its form bespeaks the study of Shakespeare. With obvious reference to his own dramatic effort Pushkin apostrophized in a letter to his friend Rayevsky:

> What is the meaning of tragedy? What is its aim? Man and the people. The destiny of man; the destiny of the people. That is why Racine is great in spite of the limiting form he imposed on his tragedy. That is why Shakespeare is great in spite of the irregularity, carelessness, and ugliness of his execution.[34]

In addition to Schiller's aesthetic influence on *Boris Godunov,* a striking topical parallel to Schiller's drama *Die Räuber* deserves to be singled out. The analogy extends to the scene in which Boris, manifesting his terror at the news of the appearance of Tsarevich Dimitry, suddenly asks of Shuysky: "Funny? ah? what? why don't you laugh?" As a matter of fact, Boris Godunov's question, "Have you ever heard that the dead return from their graves?" ending with the line quoted above, coincides almost literally with the horror-stricken exclamation of Franz Moor (V,1): "Die Toten stehen noch nicht auf. . . . Nun, warum lachst du nicht!" This correspondence was first noted by Bulgarin and later cited by Plaksin and Nadezhdin (who, however, erroneously connected it with *Kabale und Liebe*).[35]

Such a close parallel is significant and interesting because we possess relatively few data concerning the precise degree and scope of Pushkin's indebtedness to Schiller. Moreover, the picture of this tantalizing relationship is at times obscured by uncertainties, complexities, and downright dilemmas. The telltale borrowing from *Die Räuber* may well serve as an example. In April 1825, as we have mentioned before, Pushkin asked his brother to send him the *Oeuvres dramatiques de Schiller.* But the requested books were bought for him by P. A. Pletnev only in January 1826, that is, after the virtual completion of his *Boris Godunov.* The difficulty of a "borrowing" from Schiller seems almost insurmountable under these circumstances. However, the quandary may be resolved if we remember that *Boris Godunov,* due to trouble with the censor, was not permitted to appear in print until 1830. Thus Pushkin had ample time to make use of Schiller's works and plenty of opportunity to introduce into his manuscript all the deletions and additions he considered desirable.[36]

Pushkin's *chef d'oeuvre, Yevgeny Onegin* (1830), was justly acclaimed for "easiness and a lightness of style, and a picturesqueness of detail, which makes it stand unique in European literature."[37] An early draft of this singular "novel in verse" permits us to draw instructive inferences about the poet's familiarity with German literature. The lines which epitomize Onegin's literary education are particularly revealing in this respect:

> He was well versed in German letters
> Thanks to the works of Madame de Stael.

As a matter of fact, Pushkin knew and valued highly the writings of the spirited French authoress, especially her noted book. *De l'Allemagne* (1813). It thus appears reasonable to assume that these verses from *Yevgeny Onegin* constitute an autobiographical element, and that "Pushkin derived his knowledge of German literature, of Schiller and Goethe, precisely from the book *De l'Allemagne!*"[38]

There exists a theory according to which *Yevgeny Onegin* ought to be read in terms of a parody of Pushkin's juvenile poetry. An important presupposition of this theory lies in the belief that Pushkin's early literary efforts reflect to a high degree the philosophical content of Schiller's momentous poem "Die Ideale" in the renderings by Zhukovsky and Milonov.[39] To be sure, weighty and cogent reasons in support of this theory have been adduced. But even those who reject this knowledgeable conception cannot possibly close their ears to several other sonorous and suggestive echoes from Schiller in *Yevgeny Onegin.* At the outset, interest is awakened by the figure of Onegin's friend, Lensky, that "honest soul from Göttingen bowing to Kant and reading Schiller before his death."[40] In the subsequent verses one receives the impression that with Lensky's death the Russian poet actually laments the downfall of his own Schillerean aspirations.[41] This impression gains increasing strength toward the end of Chapter VI of *Yevgeny Onegin.* It is here that Pushkin voices his grief about the "withering of youth" and its "starry-eyed reveries" (VI,36), about the encroachment of "harsh reality" upon the poetic "world of the soul" (VI,43), about the "necessity of parting" with the "volatile joys of youth" (VI,45), about the inescapable surrender to the "paralyzing exigencies of life" from which he would like to escape into the realm of "surging imagination" and "poetic inspiration" (VI,46). Somehow, these wistful musings sound very familiar to the reader. In fact, a closer scrutiny reveals their striking similarity to the principal theme of Schiller's poem "Die Ideale": leave-taking from youth and youthful dreams, with work and friendship as the only guides into an uncertain future.[42]

Another signal analogy to Schiller in *Yevgeny Onegin* lies in Tatyana's farewell to the valleys, hills, and woodlands of her rural residence:

> Farewell, you peaceful valleys,
> And you, familiar hills and peaks,
> And you, familiar groves and woods;
> Farewell, you lovely skies and clouds,
> Farewell, you cheerful views of home;
> I leave my dear and quiet haunts

For urban din and gaudy glitter . . .
Farewell then, too, my independence!
What for and whither do I strive?
And what has fate for me in store?
(*Yevgeny Onegin,* VII, 28)

There can be little doubt that Tatyana's heartfelt elegy flows directly from the mighty stream of Schiller's drama, *Die Jungfrau von Orleans,* and precisely from Johanna's farewell to the beloved places of her childhood:

Lebt wohl, ihr Berge, ihr geliebten Triften,
Ihr traulich stillen Täler, lebet wohl!
Johanna wird nun nicht mehr auf euch wandeln,
Johanna sagt euch ewig Lebewohl.
Ihr Wiesen, die ich wässerte, ihr Bäume,
Die ich gepflanzet, grünet fröhlich fort!
. . . .
Ihr Plätze alle meiner stillen Freuden,
Euch lass ich hinter mir auf immerdar!
(*Die Jungfrau von Orleans,* Prolog)

Like the German poet, Pushkin was captivated by the grandiose spectacle of human history and by the deeds of exceptional leaders. In his poem *Poltava* (1829) he created an impressive panorama of the victory of Peter the Great over Charles XII of Sweden. Intertwined with the great historical drama is the passionate love of a young girl, Maria, for an old man, the Cossack traitor Mazeppa. The poem falls short of being a perfect combination of national epic and romantic narrative, but the battle scenes are depicted in the magnificent style of a fresco. There is a savage grandeur about this work:

> What an atrocious subject! Not a trace of good or noble sentiments. Not one consoling touch! Seductions, malevolence, treachery, ruse, cowardliness, cruelty. . . . What interested me was vigorous characters, and the deep, tragic shadows thrown across all those horrors.[43]

It may be a case of influence or mere coincidence, but much the same views are expressed in Schiller's treatise "Über das Erhabene" (1801):

> . . . die pathetischen Gemälde der mit dem Schicksal ringenden Menschheit, der unaufhaltsamen Flucht des Glücks, der betrogenen Sicherheit, der triumphierenden Ungerechtigkeit und der unterliegenden Unschuld, welche die Geschichte in reichem Mass aufstellt und die tragische Kunst nachahmend vor unsre Augen bringt.

As for Pushkin's "vigorous characters," the parallel to Schiller can be found in the latter's essay "Über das Pathetische" (1793):

> Wieviel mehr wir in ästhetischen Urteilen auf die Kraft als auf die Richtung der Kraft, wieviel mehr auf die Freiheit als auf Gesetzmässigkeit sehen, wird schon daraus hinlänglich offenbar, dass wir Kraft und Freiheit lieber auf Kosten der Gesetzmässigkeit geäussert, als die Gesetzmässigkeit auf Kosten der Kraft und Freiheit beobachtet sehen. . . . Ein Lasterhafter fängt an, uns zu interessieren, sobald er Glück und Leben wagen muss, um seinen schlimmen Willen durchzusetzen. . . . Rache, zum Beispiel, ist unstreitig ein unedler und selbst niedriger Affekt. Nichtsdestoweniger wird sie ästhetisch, sobald sie dem, der sie ausübt, ein schmerzhaftes Opfer kostet.

In 1830 Pushkin began work on a satire aimed at the Russian serf system, *A History of the Village of Goryukhino,* which he left unfinished. But two years later he took up the same subject matter in his tale *Dubrovsky.* It is the tragic story of a young nobleman turned brigand in order to revenge his father, who had been ruined by a powerful magnate. The analogy to Schiller's drama *Die Räuber,* especially to the figure of Karl Moor, seems at close quarters. On the other hand, it must be admitted that "the tradition of the idealized or noble-minded brigand, from Schiller's Karl Moor to *Jean Sbogar* by Charles Nodier, was still strong at the time, not to mention Pushkin's old interest in the Volga bandits."[44]

The Polish uprising in November 1830 came as a profound shock to Pushkin, the friend and admirer of Adam Mickiewicz.[45] The "bad news" from Warsaw instilled dismay and sorrow into his loyal Russian heart. Rarely, during that unhappy period, was there anything to brighten his life. However, in the spring of 1831, Pushkin wrote to his friend P. A. Vyazemsky: "Here is a piece of good news for you: Zhukovsky has just completed twelve marvellous ballads and a great number of other wonderful things."[46] Pushkin's joy, to be exact, was caused by Zhukovsky's masterly renderings of twelve of Schiller's ballads including "Klage der Ceres," "Das Siegesfest," "Der Kampf mit dem Drachen," and others. On June 11, 1831, the poet again addressed a letter to Vyazemsky indicative of his continual interest in Zhukovsky's translations and his preoccupation with the revolutionary war in Poland:

> Zhukovsky keeps writing without interruption. He has translated several ballads by Southey, Schiller, and Uhland; among other things "The Diver," "The Glove," "The Ring of Polycrates," and so forth. . . . In the present bitter circumstances there is nothing else that can give us comfort.[47]

In the fall of 1831 Pushkin received a letter from F. N. Glinka which contributed, albeit modestly, to expanding his knowledge concerning the German poet:

> Even if I had forgotten you my wife would have reminded me of you. To be explicit, she placed your portrait next to Schiller's and Goethe's. I must tell you that in her maiden years she translated an entire volume of Schiller's. Yesterday I tore out a page from her manuscript and I am herewith sending you the "War Song" from *Wallenstein's Camp.*[48]

About the year 1835 Pushkin considered writing a prose drama, *Scenes from Feudal Times,* a trenchant project which —unfortunately—never materialized. All that has come down to us is a succinct outline scribbled in French reminiscent of Schiller's dramas *Wilhelm Tell* and *Demetrius.* The brevity of the draft does not permit much speculation as to

Pushkin's ultimate dramaturgical intentions, but we can surmise that he envisioned a "highly concentrated drama of realistic mass movement" modeled after the superb mass scenes in the plays of Schiller.[49] Comparable to the creative efforts of Goethe and Schiller, Pushkin's literary activities branched out into the sphere of journalism. In 1836 he founded his own periodical, *Sovremennik (The Contemporary)*, and before long gave evidence of being a spirited and quick-witted publicist. This "deviation" from pure and honest "literature" prompted several St. Petersburg magazines to launch a series of bitter attacks on the unsuspecting poet. One of the derogators went so far as to declare: "Pushkin is no longer a poet for the reason that he publishes a journal."[50] It was V. F. Odoyevsky who stood up in defense of "the Russian poet Pushkin":

> It would be ludicrous to object to such an accusation. Moreover, it would be an insult to the reader if we ventured to remind him of the fact that Karamzin and Zhukovsky, Schiller and Goethe were journalists. . . . Pushkin has not come to a dead end on his journey, gentlemen, as it so often happens with our littérateurs: just as Goethe and Schiller, he knows how to read, work, and think.[51]

When M. Ye. Lobanov, an implacable foe of the French revolution, rode full tilt against certain contemporary writers, "corrupting youth and infecting them with criminal tendencies" (probably an allusion to such works as *Die Räuber* and "The Robber Brothers"), Pushkin was quick to rebut the charges in his *Sovremennik* (1836):

> Presumably, Schiller did not write his *Robbers* with a view to calling the young out of the universities and onto the highways. Why then imply criminal intentions in our present-day writers when their works can clearly be interpreted as desiring to engage and enchant the imagination of the reader?[52]

Pushkin wrote these lines in defense of Schiller (and, perhaps, in defense of his own artistic principles), a short time before he became entangled in his fateful "affair of honor." Oddly enough, he had been warned to beware of a "white man." When he faced his destiny he may have thought of that premonition:

> His [d'Anthès's] coat was half open and showed the white Horse Guardsman's uniform he was wearing. Could it have been that at that moment Pushkin thought of the old German fortune-teller's prediction? She had warned him to beware of a "white man": a *weisser Mensch.* There the white man was. And Pushkin was about to fight him.[53]

Pushkin lost his life in this unnecessary duel. But "a Posa does not die for a little boy." The true reason was poignantly formulated by another great Russian poet: "In reality, Pushkin was not at all killed by Dantès's bullet; in reality, he was killed by the lack of fresh air. With him died his culture."[54]

What conclusions can be drawn from this scrutiny of Pushkin's attitude toward German literature? According to the customary view, Pushkin's poetic development occurred under the ascendancy of French and English writers. In contrast to this view, we have arrived at the proposition that German literature, too, and Schiller in particular, made substantial contributions to his poetic growth. As early as his student days at Tsarskoye Selo, he had been introduced to German literature. Mainly through the efforts and the enthusiasm of his schoolmates Küchelbecker and Delvig he awakened to the poetry of Klopstock, Schiller, and Goethe.[55] A great many of Pushkin's early verses show in consequence distinct traces of Schiller's poetry, notably of "Die Ideale," which he read in the renderings by Milonov and Zhukovsky and, perhaps, also in the original.[56]

But, as we have seen, Schiller's influence was not limited to the youthful efforts of the Russian poet. Throughout the years of his maturity—from the "Robber Brothers" over *Boris Godunov* to *Yevgeny Onegin*—the author of "Die Ideale" remained his faithful companion and a source of poetic inspiration. It is Pushkin himself who acknowledges his indebtedness to Schiller in *Yevgeny Onegin,* his crowning achievement, by ironizing his Schillerean *juvenilia* and by immersing the figure of Lensky in the dark waters of Schiller's sagacious, delusionless lyricism. Chapter VI with its detailed reelaboration of all the motifs of "Die Ideale" is most revealing in this regard. Not to be overlooked, finally, are the concluding lines of *Yevgeny Onegin* which overflow with reminiscences from Schiller's elegy:

> Farewell, you too, my strange companion,
> And you, ideals fair and true,
> And you, continual and soulful
> Though humble toil. With you I knew
> All that a poet can desire:
> Oblivion in the storms of life,
> The sweet loquacity of friends.
> (*Yevgeny Onegin,* VIII, 50)

Thus, very poignantly, Pushkin's masterpiece terminates with the last inferences of Schiller's elegy "Die Ideale": with a tender and melancholy withdrawal from the exalted illusions of youth to the sober bastions of work and friendship.[57]

To delve into the intricacies of Pushkin's relationship with Goethe is an intriguing and challenging task. Western researchers have tended to focus on his writings and paid scant attention to the details of his upbringing, environment, and general cultural atmosphere of the capital. His family's love of French language and culture combined with his father's contempt of German letters were bound to leave an impression on Pushkin's mind and development. Eventually, he had to depend on translations, Russian periodicals, and Mme de Stael's *De l'Allemagne* to inform himself about the state and progress of German literature.

In the presence of such a powerful pro-French trend it is surprising to note the increasing number of Pushkin's references to Goethe, especially after the completion of his

Boris Godunov in 1825. What is more, this interest in the German poet was not stimulated by a pilgrimage to Weimar as, for instance, in the case of Shevyryov, Grech, Glinka, Zhukovsky and many others. It was kindled by Goethe's dramatic achievements exemplified by *Götz von Berlichingen* and *Faust.* So overwhelmed was the Russian poet by the mighty creation of *Faust* that he assumed before it an attitude of stunned reverence and prostration comparing its author to Homer, Dante, Shakespeare, Molière—and even the Holy Spirit. Of course, the last comparison amounted to a blasphemy in the eyes of the authorities and furnished them with a pretext to exile the culprit to his mother's estate, Mikhaylovskoye, near Pskov.

Pushkin's admiration for the author of *Faust* has left distinct traces in his own poetic works. Hermann, for example, the hero of *The Queen of Spades,* bears a great resemblance to Goethe's Mephistopheles. The caustic and destructive tendency of Goethe's devil finds a close parallel in certain wicked traits of Eugene Onegin, too. The high point of literary affinity is perhaps reached in Pushkin's poem "The Demon" where the evil spirit stages a spectacular comeback in Russian disguise. André von Gronicka speaks in this connection of "significant influence by Goethe on Pushkin" and "a clear case of 'borrowing.' "[58] One is tempted to say the same of Pushkin's *Scene from Faust.* At the first glance it looks like a reflection or copy of Goethe's *Faust* and the analogy appears to reach the point of identity or far-ranging imitation. Like in the German work, Pushkin's protagonists, Faust and Mephistopheles, carry on an argument about Margarete's future. Similar to his German prototype, Pushkin's Faust abandons himself to bittersweet memories of love and its irretrievable ecstasies and is brutally awakened from his reveries by the sardonic remarks of the devil.

To be sure, these are striking analogies—and yet Pushkin's Faust turns out to be very different from his German model. He emerges as a victim of Mephistopheles who apparently has succeeded in destroying in his heart all productive impulses and higher aspirations. Pushkin's Faust experiences no thirst for knowledge, nor is he able to restore his physical and mental strength by living in harmony with nature. Instead of ascending like Goethe's Faust, he is hopelessly falling into an abyss of listless apathy, a prey of the hellborn *taedium vitae.*

At this juncture a question may arise as to Pushkin's motivation for contriving his desolate and desperate *Scene from Faust.* It seems this question can best be answered by pointing to the state of spiritual crisis in which Pushkin was engulfed at the time of composing the *Scene from Faust* (1826). He himself, as a man and poet, felt threatened by the demon of doubt and cynicism and imperceptibly drawn into the mire of world-weariness, of spiritual and artistic extinction. As a protection, he projected his innermost anguish into the figure of Faust thus, in a creative way (after the fashion of Goethe), emancipating himself from the spirit of negation.

Pushkin's portrayal of Faust as a victim of existential boredom precipitated a thematic chain reaction in Russian and world literature. Thanks to the artistry of this representation Pushkin's necromancer became the fountain-head of an impressive clan of literary descendants: Lermontov's Pechorin, Goncharov's Oblomov, Turgenev's Rudin, Tolstoy's Vronsky and, of course, his own Eugene Onegin. All these sensitive but "superfluous men" sustain the torturous burden of boredom, the very same irremediable misery by which Pushkin's Faust is afflicted. Conceiving of boredom as an ontological disease and transposing it into the redeeming realm of literature the Russian poet inaugurated a line of thought that leads from Leopardi and Kierkegaard over Schopenhauer and Heidegger to Sartre's *La Nausée* and Moravia's *La noia.*

Toward the end of Pushkin's *Scene* Faust's disgust with humanity reaches such a point that he orders the devil to wreck a ship. This is reminiscent of the Philemon and Baucis scene in Goethe's *Faust* where Mephisto is ordered to demolish the house of the old couple. On the surface both commands seem equally cruel and senseless. But the difference lies in the particular that Goethe's Faust acts to promote the "happiness of future generations" whereas Pushkin's Faust is driven by a demonic distaste for "all that exists."

In substance, the *Scene from Faust* illustrates the impact of the mature Goethe on the Russian poet. Pushkin's *Boris Godunov,* by contrast, reflects the *Storm and Stress* tendencies of the young Goethe: crass realism, topical atmosphere, and historical costume. To pinpoint specific instances of this influence seems a Sisyphean task. Scholars have been hard put to distinguish between the influence of the German and the influence of Shakespeare to whom both Goethe and Pushkin are indebted.

All these analogies and parallels are indicative of Pushkin's increasing affinity with the creator of *Götz* and *Faust.* But if the Russian's individuality is to be appreciated the crucial differences between him and the German poet must be thrown into relief. Very revealing in this respect is their particular conception of mankind. The sage of Weimar thought of humanity as a manifestation of nature while Pushkin held the belief that it was a product of history. In keeping with this belief the Russian did not feel any urge to investigate the physical world as it was envisioned and practiced by Goethe nor did he ever attempt to elaborate a cosmology or philosophy of nature. Such a disparity in personality and outlook was bound to exercise a restraining influence on Goethe's ascendancy over the Russian poet. At least in part it may account for the greater measure of inspiration Pushkin was able to draw from Walter Scott, Byron, and Shakespeare. And yet, in spite of all, Goethe's influence was growing steadily, though slowly, during the last years of Pushkin's life.

It would seem idle to speculate on the form and outcome of a literary relationship that was cut short by the untimely death of the Russian. Judging from its promising initial development it might have ripened into a rich harvest of inspired works. Even so, merely on the narrow basis of the adduced examples, Pushkin's attitude toward Goethe can be aptly described as a blend of creative reception and awe-struck acclaim. It was the evil figure of Mephisto which made him realize his own ominous affinity with the spirit of destruction and thus prepared the way for his redemption. This is certainly a striking illustration of Goethe's impact on Pushkin, especially in view of its important personal and poetic consequences and the successful reestablishment of his spiritual equilibrium. Pushkin's creative assimilation of Goethe's poetry together with his untiring admiration for the author of *Faust,* that "mightiest creation" and "beacon of modern times," leave us with the impression that to him the German poet was really far more than "just a distant and but vaguely perceived figure."[59]

Pushkin's rank has been firmly established in Russian letters. His difficulty in attaining a paramount place in world literature derives from the intrinsic untranslatability of his prodigious works.[60] With the possible exception of *Boris Godunov* and *Yevgeny Onegin,* which for the most part are known only in the musical settings by Mussorgsky and Tchaikovsky, the foreign reader is commonly unaware of the originality and vitality of his achievements. Under these circumstances, the intermediary and interpretive role of comparative literature cannot be overestimated. The critical need for comparative studies in the field of Pushkin scholarship was effectively epitomized in a review article by J. Thomas Shaw:

> Pushkin belongs to world literature, and comparative studies are still needed to show, not only how writers of other times and countries have reacted to Pushkin, but also how he reacted to writers and their works of various times and nationalities. Perhaps both Soviet and Western scholars could profit by dialogue.[61]

Notes

INTRODUCTION

1. O. P. Peterson, *Schiller in Russland* (New York, 1934; vol. II, New York, 1939); Katharina Schütz, *Das Goethebild Turgeniews* (Bern, 1952); Nils Ake Nilsson, *Ibsen in Russland* (Stockholm, 1958); Charles Passage, *The Russian Hoffmannists* (The Hague, 1963); Natalie Reber, *Studien zum Motiv des Doppelgängers bei Dostojevskij und E. T. A. Hoffmann* (Giessen, 1964); Edmund Kostka, *Schiller in Russian Literature* (Philadelphia, 1965); Gerhard Kersten, *Gerhart Hauptmann und Lev Nikolajevič Tolstoj* (Wiesbaden, 1966); K. E. Laage, *Theodor Storm und Iwan Turgenjew* (Heide, 1967); André von Gronicka, *The Russian Image of Goethe* (Philadelphia, 1968); H. B. Harder, *Schiller in Russland* (Bad Homburg, 1969); Hans Erich Brand, *Kleist und Dostojevskij* (Bonn, 1970).

2. S. Durylin, "Russkie pisateli u Gete v Veimare," *Literaturnoye Nasledstvo* IV–VI (Moskva, 1932), pp. 81–504; V. Zhirmunsky, *Gete v russkoy literature* (Leningrad, 1937); E. Winter, *Halle als Ausgangspunkt der deutschen Russlandkunde* (Berlin, 1953); E. Reissner, *Alexander Herzen in Deutschland* (Berlin, 1963); H. Raab, *Die Lyrik Puškins in Deutschland* (Berlin, 1964); G. Ziegengeist, ed., *I. S. Turgenjew und Deutschland* (Berlin, 1965); H. Grasshoff, *A. D. Kantemir und West-Europa* (Berlin, 1966); U. Lehmann, *Der Gottschedkreis und Russland* (Berlin, 1966); W. Krauss, ed., *Slawisch-deutsche Wechselseitigkeit in Sprache, Literatur und Kultur* (Berlin, 1968).

3. Alois Hofman, *Thomas Mann und die Welt der russischen Literatur* (Berlin, 1967), p. 23. See also my review of Hofman's book in *Rivista di Letterature Moderne e Comparate,* XXIII (December 1970), 314–16.

4. Cf. B. V. Varneke, *History of the Russian Theater* (New York, 1951), p. 67 ff. and p. 71 ff.

5. Cf. D. Chizhevsky, *Gegel v Rossii* (Paris, 1939), and *Hegel bei den Slaven* (Bad Homburg, 1961); W. Setschkareff, *Schellings Einfluss in der russischen Literatur* (Leipzig, 1939).

6. For details see E. Kostka, *Schiller in Russian Literature,* p. 24 ff. and p. 135 ff.

7. Very popular at the time were K. Nötzel, *Das Leben Dostojewskis* (Leipzig, 1925), and J. Meier-Graefe, *Dostojewski, der Dichter* (Berlin, 1926).

8. Tamara L. Motylyova, *O mirovom znachenii L. N. Tolstogo* (Moskva, 1957), p. 585–87.

9. Surprisingly, it is not Böll the novelist or dramatist but rather Böll the lyric poet who has found a sympathetic reception in the Soviet Union. The Soviet Germanist Lev Kopelev has recently emerged as one of the most sensitive and knowledgeable interpreters of the German writer. Cf. *Die Zeit* (July 20, 1971), p. 9–10. Cf. also Kopelev's *Zwei Epochen deutsch-russischer Literaturbeziehungen* (Frankfurt, 1973), p. 95.

CHAPTER 1: FYODOR SOLOGUB AND HEINRICH MANN

1. Cf., A. von Gronicka, "Thomas Mann and Russia," *The Stature of Thomas Mann,* ed. Charles Neider (New York, 1947), pp. 307–25; E. Schober, *Thomas Mann und Tolstoj* (Göttingen, 1950); L. Venohr, *Thomas Manns Verhältnis zur russischen Literatur* (Meisenheim/Glan, 1959); Alois Hofman, *Thomas Mann und die Welt der russischen Literatur* (Berlin, 1967).

2. Fyodor Sologub, *Sobr. Soch.* (St. Petersburg, n.d.), VI, 110. All translations are mine.

3. Sologub, *Sobr. Soch.*, p. 111. Cf. Renato Poggioli, *The Poets of Russia* (Cambridge, Mass., 1960), p. 107: ". . .Peredonov is another provincial schoolmaster, representing not only the mire of life, but also the filth of the soul."

4. Sologub, *Sobr. Soch.*, p. 15. Cf. Poggioli, *The Poets of Russia,* p. 87: "The Decadent poet remains alone in his misery, as he was in his glory, precisely because he is deprived of a sense of human fellowship."

5. Heinrich Mann, *Gesammelte Romane* (Leipzig, 1917), VI, 45. Hereafter abridged to *G. R.*

6. H. Mann, *G. R.*, p. 191. With reference to *Professor Unrat,* Fritz Martini speaks in this connection of "neuromantischer Rausch der Nerven" and "komödiantenhaftamoralisches Ästhetentum" in *Deutsche Literaturgeschichte* (Stuttgart, 1952), p. 490.

7. Cf. *O F. Sologube Kritika,* ed. A. Chebotarevskaya (St. Petersburg, 1911), pp. 349–50.

8. H. Mann, *G. R.*, p. 10.

9. *Ibid.*, pp. 13, 17, 22.

10. *Ibid.*, p. 49.

11. *Ibid.*, p. 32.

12. *Ibid.*, p. 277.

13. *Ibid.*, p. 180.

14. *Ibid.*, p. 44, 45, 199.

15. *Ibid.*, pp. 48, 172.

16. Hermann Sinsheimer, *Heinrich Manns Werk* (München, 1921), pp. 29, 30. Cf. Paul Fechter, *Geschichte der deutschen Literatur* (Gütersloh, 1952), p. 520: "Es ist Satire, die sich . . . ihr Objekt erst selber schafft und darum ins Unwirkliche statt in die Wirklichkeit stösst."

17. Pieter Boonstra, *Heinrich Mann als politischer Schriftsteller* (Utrecht, 1945), p. 132.

18. *O Sologube Kritika*, p. 60.

19. *Ibid.*, p. 152. Cf. Poggioli, *The Poets of Russia*, p. 110: "Sologub feels indeed that 'only children are alive,' while adults 'have been dead for long.' It will be recalled that Dostoyevsky and Blok ("I love only art, children, and death.") held very similar views.

20. H. Mann, *G. R.*, p. 262.

21. *Ibid.*, p. 90.

22. *Ibid.*, p. 270. Sologub wrote a play, *Hostages of Life.* As a playwright he is indebted to Ibsen, Hauptmann, and Maeterlinck.

23. F. Sologub, *Sobr. Soch.* (St. Petersburg, 1913), XIII, 124. Cf. Poggioli, *The Poets of Russia*, p. 85: "Sologub raised to the level of an apotheosis this coarse worship of the self: 'I am perfect, I am the only God.' "

24. H. Mann, *Die Göttinnen* (Berlin, 1932), pp. 430, 685; see also *O Sologube Kritika*, p. 218.

25. Sologub, *Sobr. Soch.*, VI, 328–29. It appears that the "romanische Kultur der Sinne und Ekstasen" (Martini, *Deutsche Literatur-geschichte*, p. 489) was not at all a prerogative of the Romance countries but that it flourished in the Slavic East with equal exuberance.

26. Cf. *O Sologube Kritika*, p. 20. But cf. W. Harkins, *Dictionary of Russian Literature* (New York, 1956), p. 381: "The Sasha-Lyudmila episode, though intended as a contrast to the evil of Peredonov's life, is a failure."

27. Sologub, *Sobr. Soch.*, VI, 313; Poggioli, *The Poets of Russia*, p. 84: Peredonov's destiny was also the historic destiny of Sologub and his peers: "Wanderers in a starless sky, seekers after a somber paradise, we trusted in our path, and dreamed of the lights of heaven. Yet we stopped at the threshold, heavy with shame and anguish. . . ."

28. *O. Sologube Kritika*, p. 75.

29. *Ibid.*, p. 76. The idea that the sufferings of innocent children must be justified looms large in Dostoyevsky's novel *The Brothers Karamazov.*

30. *Ibid.*, p. 77. This is, in essence, the agonizing question of Ivan Karamazov and the reason of his struggle with God the Creator.

31. H. Mann, *G. R.*, VI, 196.

32. *Ibid.*, p. 81.

33. *Ibid.*, p. 276.

34. Sinsheimer, *Heinrich Manns Werk*, pp. 28, 29. In contrast to this, Fechter sees in Unrat a "verknöcherten Oberlehrer . . . der ausbricht . . . wie ein Balzacscher Besessener durch das Laster tobt und doch ein Bürger bleibt." *Geschichte der deutschen Literatur*, p. 520.

35. H. Mann, *Macht und Mensch* (München, 1919), p. 19.

36. H. Mann, *G. R.*, VI, 35.

37. Sologub, *Sobr. Soch.*, VI, 2. Cf. Ivan Tkhorzhevsky: "His novel *The Little Demon* continues Gogol's epic of triviality, the *Dead Souls*. But Gogol saw a ray of light before him. Sologub sees before him only death." Ivan Tkhorzhevsky, *Russkaya Literatura* (Paris, 1950), p. 474. Sologub's *taedium vitae*, his morbid aversion for life are reminiscent of the hopeless pessimism of Giacomo Leopardi. It might be interesting and worthwhile to devote a comparative study to these two poets.

38. *O Sologube Kritika*, p. 64.

39. Arthur Luther, "Fedor Sologub," *Osteuropa* III (Berlin, 1927–28), 304.

40. *O Sologube Kritika*, pp. 307, 340. Cf. also D. S. Mirsky, *A History of Russian Literature* (New York, 1949), p. 444.

41. *O Sologube Kritika*, p. 203. Tkhorzhevsky, however, holds a less high opinion of Sologub: "Sologub—a talented, remarkable poet. He has become in Russian literature the singer of 'My Father, the Devil' and himself the father of *The Little Demon*. But withal he has remained—as befits a servant of lie—preeminently a deceiver, a mystifier." *Russkaya Literatura*, p. 473.

42. Sinsheimer, *Heinrich Manns Werk*, p. 31.

43. *Ibid.*, p. 28.

44. Some modern critics such as Paul Fechter have taken exception to *Professor Unrat* denouncing its "zeitbedingte Verkrampftheit." *Geschichte der deutschen Literatur*, p. 520.

45. Cf. *O Sologube kritika*, p. 330. In his "yearning for beauty" Heinrich Mann emerges as a spiritual twin-brother of Sologub. In this connection cf. Ettore Lo Gatto, *Storia della Letteratura Russa* (Firenze, 1944), p. 496.

46. F. Sologub, *The Little Demon* (New York, 1916), p. xv. Tkhorzhevsky has pointed out that Peredonov is, in fact, "no one else but Chekhov's 'Man in a Shell' who has crept out of his shell and attempts to hide in the shell the entire world together with the sun. Also the sun is to Sologub a Peredonov, only a gigantic one—the fiery embodiment of universal vulgarity, Saltykov's triumphing swine, and simultaneously a spectre, the 'grey Nedotykomka' (bluish, impudent, horrible, bloody and stinking)." *Russkaya Literatura*, p. 474.

47. Cf. A. von Gronicka, "Thomas Mann and Russia," pp. 307, 309; see also von Gronicka's recent study, *Thomas Mann: Profile and Perspectives* (New York, 1970), which abounds in references to Russian literature.

48. Vyacheslav Ivanov, *Po zvezdam* (St. Petersburg, 1909), p. 87. It is interesting to note that Heinrich Mann's affinity with Fyodor Sologub has been ignored by the experts in East and West. Cf., for instance, Ulrich Weisstein, *Heinrich Mann: Eine historisch-kritische Einführung in sein dichterisches Werk* (Tübingen, 1962). T. Motylyova mentions only a possible influence of L. Tolstoy's treatise *The Kingdom*

of Heaven Is Within Us (1891–93) on H. Mann's *Der Untertan* (1911). Cf. "Leo Tolstoj und die deutsche Literatur," *Kunst und Literatur* XI–XII (Berlin, 1960), 1116 ff. This would be a strange case of literary influence for Tolstoy's central theme in his treatise is "nonresistance to evil."

CHAPTER 2: GORKY

1. Yu. Yuzovsky, *Maksim Gorky i yego dramaturgia* (Moskva, 1959), p. 452; George Lukacs, *Der russische Realismus in der Weltliteratur* (Berlin, 1964), II, 406. The depreciatory view was expressed by Renato Poggioli, *The Poets of Russia* (Cambridge, Mass., 1960), p. 3; very harsh also the verdict of Vsevolod Setschkareff, *Geschichte der russischen Literatur* (Stuttgart, 1966), p. 136.

2. Yuzovsky, *Maksim Gorky i yego dramaturgia,* p. 443. Lukacs speaks of Gorky's "tendency to glorify romantically the world of the vagabonds." *Der russische Realismus in der Weltliteratur,* p. 34.

3. *M. Gorky—Materialy i issledovania* (Moskva-Leningrad, 1936), II, 164.

4. *Ibid.*, III, 196.

5. F.P. Schiller, *Fridrikh Schiller* (Moskva, 1955), p. 10. Gorky's affinity with Schiller comes to light in the second part of his autobiography *(Among Strange People).* The finale savors of Schiller's poem "An die Freude," specifically in its dithyrambic motifs of joy, festive dance, brotherhood, and love. Also Gorky's early plays are reminiscent of the German's "family dramas" and "philosophical tragedies." Gorky cherished the "fiery words of Schiller" in *Kabale und Liebe,* which he described as a "most beautiful and romantic play." Cf. Boris A. Byalik, *M. Gorky—literaturny kritik* (Moskva, 1960), p. 15.

6. Cf. L. Tolstoy's letter to M.N. Korengold of November 10, 1902. It was in Nizhni Novgorod (1889) that the student N.S. Vasilyev initiated Gorky into the ideas of Nietzsche. One result was the figure of Jacob Mayakin in the novel *Foma Gordeyev* (1899) whose views bear resemblance to the concepts of Nietzsche. Also Satin's discourse on the "dignity of Man" in the drama *The Lower Depths* (1902) rumbles with the heavy pathos of the German philosopher. In his "Talks about the Trade" (1930) Gorky belatedly disclaimed any infatuation with the "social philosophy of Friedrich Nietzche." Cf. M. Gorky, *Sobr. soch.* (Moskva, 1949–55), XXV, 320–321.

7. Yuzovsky, *Maksim Gorky i yego dramaturgia,* p. 444.

8. *Ibid.*, p. 453. See also N. Moravcevich, "Gorky and the Western Naturalists," *Comparative Literature* XXI (1969), 63–75. The Gorky-Ibsen-Hauptmann relationship and the question of Gorky's stature are analyzed. Gorky is seen not as a "naturalist" but rather as a "romanticist."

9. Yuzovsky, *Maksim Gorky i yego dramaturgia,* p. 467–68.

10. *Ibid.*, pp. 469–70. Gorky was acquainted with Hauptmann's *Hannele;* he mentions it in his article "Paul Verlaine and the Decadents" (1896).

11. *Ibid.*, p. 477. *Yegor Bulychov* had its West-European première in Switzerland in 1973. Cf. *Die Zeit* (June 29, 1973) p. 11.

12. Gorky, *Sobr. soch.*, XXIX, 456. In this respect, Gorky resembled Lenin, who also cherished a belief that suffering was not an indispensable part of life. Cf. A. Lavretsky, *Esteticheskie vzglyady russkikh pisateley* (Moskva, 1963), p. 276. For Gorky's relationship with Lenin see Bertram D. Wolfe, *The Bridge and the Abyss: The Troubled Friendship of Maxim Gorky and V. I. Lenin* (New York, 1967).

13. Gorky's *Lower Depths* appears to have inspired O'Neill's drama *The Iceman Cometh* (1939), which shows a number of correspondences both in subject matter and composition: "One might describe it [*The Iceman Cometh*] as a *Lower Depths* written with psychological complexity as well as with flashes of anger and scorn." John Gassner, *Masters of the Drama* (New York, 1954), p. 735.

14. Referring to *A Confession*, Byalik speaks of Gorky's "detachment from reality and revolutionary action," *M. Gorky—literaturny kritik*, p. 36. N. Ludwig cites in this connection Gorky's "ideological and political errors" which aroused the ire of Lenin. Cf. *Maxim Gorki* (Berlin, 1968), p. 149. It is interesting to note that the Bible was a source of poetic inspiration also to B. Brecht. See the informative article of Thomas Brandt, "Brecht und die Bibel," *PMLA* LXXIX (March 1964), 171–76.

15. Gorky, *Sobr. soch.*, XXIV, 33–34. Gorky lived on Capri from 1906 to 1913. It is difficult to imagine that he was not familiar with the remarkable religious and poetic achievements of St. Francis of Assisi.

16. *Ibid.*

17. *Ibid.*, p. 526. These are lines which were later discarded by Gorky.

18. *Ibid.*, p. 36.

19. *Ibid.*, XXIX, 156. Letter to P. Kh. Maksimov of January 31, 1911. Gorky recommended the study of Balzac, Flaubert, Stendhal, Maupassant, Schiller, Byron, Shelley, Scott, Dickens, and others. In addition, Gorky almost "raved" about Rostand's *Cyrano* while taking exception to Zola's "unforgivable naturalism." Cf. Byalik, *M. Gorky—literaturny kritik*, pp. 29, 84.

20. Gorky, *Sobr. soch.*, XXIX, 303–4.

21. *M. Gorky—Materialy i issledovania*, II, 164. The quotation is from Gorky's article "Two Souls" (1915), which recently was denounced by Soviet critics for characterizing the West as "active" and the East as "passive." Cf. Lavretsky, *Esteticheskie vzglyady russkikh pisateley*, pp. 269–70.

22. Gorky, *Sobr. soch.*, XXIX, 585.

23. "The 'Serapion Brothers' received only a grudging blessing from above under the quasi-official label of 'revolutionary Romanticism,' which Gorky had once invented as a political justification for some aspects of his work." Poggioli, *The Poets of Russia*, p. 295. It was one of the ironies of his life that Gorky himself discovered and sponsored these promising young poets with whom he later, in the years of the "personality cult," was compelled to collide *ex officio*, that is, as President of the Union of Soviet Writers. Cf. Richard R. Sheldon, "Šklovskij, Gor'kij, and the Serapion Brothers," *The Slavic & East European Journal* XII (Spring 1968), 1–13.

24. Irwin Weil, *Gorky* (New York, 1966), p. 22. In December 1917 Gorky wrote

an article in the periodical *Novaya Zhizn'* in which he charged that the communists regarded Russia as "experimental material" and that the proletariat would suffer grievously from this "most wicked experiment." Counterattacking, the communists denounced Gorky for "underestimating the proletariat and overestimating the bourgeois intelligentsia" (Ludwig, *Maxim Gorki,* p. 195). These and other "fundamental disagreements" may have contributed to Gorky's decision to leave the Soviet Union in 1921 and live in Fascist Italy until 1928. In 1922 Gorky published in Germany a brochure about the Russian peasantry (never republished in the Soviet Union), in which he expressed his horror at the "sadistic and savage cruelties" committed equally by Whites and Reds during the civil war. He even voiced doubts that Russia could "ever be rescued from the slough of barbarism into which it had sunk." Cf. Weil, *Gorky,* p. 25.

25. Weil, *Gorky,* p. 116.

26. Gorky gave material assistance to many intellectuals during the first years after the revolution. Utilizing his prestige, he obtained food ration cards for the starving writers and lucrative employment in publishing houses and cultural institutions. Despite his lifelong interest in the problems of translating Gorky did not translate himself (except two poems). He encouraged others to produce high-quality renderings of foreign masterpieces in the belief that "translations were a means of bringing the peoples closer to one another." Cf. *Mezhdunarodnye svyazi russkoy literatury,* ed. M.P. Alekseyev (Moskva, 1963), pp. 60–61.

27. Cf. B.V. Mikhaylovsky, *Tvorchestvo Gorkogo i mirovaya literatura* (Moskva, 1965), p. 79. According to Otto P. Peterson, a Russian actor once made the following comparisom between Gorky and Schiller: "Although Schiller died one hundred years ago he remains (in the eyes of the bureaucrats) a rebellious individual—even more dangerous than Gorki (after Schiller the most oppressed dramatist)." *Schiller in Russland* (New York, 1934), p. 309.

28. Gorky, *Sobr. soch.,* XXIV, 257.

29. *Ibid.,* p. 355. Gorky refers to Schiller's poem "Die Weltweisen":

> Einstweilen bis den Bau der Welt
> Philosophie zusammenhält,
> Erhält sie [die Natur] das Getriebe
> Durch Hunger und durch Liebe.

30. *Ibid.,* p. 475. As for *The Robbers,* Gorky reproached the old Karamazov for not having read the dramas of Schiller with sufficient attention: "The older brothers Karamazov had their spiritual brothers among the German youth of the eighteenth century, and if father Karamazov had attentively read Schiller's dramas *Don Carlos* and *The Robbers* he would have been able to understand his children incomparably better than he actually did." *Ibid.,* XXVI, 167. Gorky regarded Dostoyevsky as an "evil genius" and said he would prefer "that the 'civilized world' would unite not under Dostoyevsky but under Pushkin, for the

colossal and universal talent of Pushkin was a psychologically healthy and salutary one." *Ibid.*, XXV. 252.

31. *Ibid.*, XXVI, 170. Gorky mentions also Byron, Leopardi, Lenau, and Baudelaire, among others, who were infected by this "mood of hopelessness." Yet as a young man Gorky was fascinated by the patriotic poetry of Leopardi. The last part of Gorky's poem "The Girl and Death" (1892) is reminiscent of Leopardi's poem "Love and Death." The difference consists in the nuance that Gorky views death not as a liberator from suffering but rather as an instrument and servant of life. Cf. Mikhaylovsky, *Tvorchestvo Gorkogo i mirovaya literatura,* pp. 16, 30, 44.

32. *Ibid.*, p. 49.

33. In the German original: "Im Anfang war die Tat." The following item concerning Goethe's *Faust* may be adduced as a curiosity: "Much publicity was given to Stalin's handwritten statement on Gorky's tale 'Death and the Girl,' that the simple legend was 'stronger than Goethe's *Faust.*' " Weil, *Gorky,* p. 129.

34. Gorky, *Sobr. soch.*, XXIX, 303–4.

35. *Ibid.*, XXVI, 421.

36. Lukacs, *Der russische Realismus in der Weltliteratur,* p. 16.

37. Gorky, *Sobr. soch.*, XXVI, 420.

38. Weil, *Gorky,* p. 127. The Union of Soviet Writers was founded in 1932 by decree of the Central Committee of the Communist Party. The First Congress was held in 1934. Gorky was its initiator, organizer, and first president. In his inaugural address on August 17, 1934, Gorky stressed the importance of work for the development of human civilization. In literature he envisioned an artistic portrayal of reality based on the epic and heroic aspects of life. In other words, he established the principles of a new kind of Soviet literature, the so-called "Socialist Realism." Cf. also Byalik, *M. Gorky—literaturny kritik,* p. 84.

39. There can be little doubt that the doctrine of "Socialist Realism" must be blamed for suppressing some of the most exciting developments in Soviet cultural life. Suffice it to mention the phenomenal vitality of Russian poetry during the first quarter of the twentieth century—from Blok to Pasternak. The contrast between this period of artistic bloom and the barrenness of the Stalinist era is so striking that any comment seems superfluous. Cf. Weil, *Gorky,* p. 129.

40. Gorky, *Sobr. soch.*, XXVI, 358. Gorky here becomes guilty of gross exaggeration by identifying one or two Fascist countries with the "world beyond the frontiers of the Soviet Union."

41. Weil, *Gorky,* p. 151.

42. According to the editor, A.I. Ovcharenko, the new edition will include "every line written by Gorky." It remains to be seen if, for instance, Gorky's articles from *Novaya Zhizn'* (1917–18), which are boldly critical of the Bolsheviks and of Lenin, will be reprinted in their entirety from first to last. Fortunately, an English translation of these challenging essays has been made available by Herman Ermolaev: *Maxim Gorky—Untimely Thoughts: Essays on Revolution, Culture and the Bolsheviks 1917–1918,* (New York, 1968).

43. Byalik, *M. Gorky—literaturny kritik,* p. 81. It is significant, however, that in the greater part of his works Gorky deals with the bourgeois past rather than with the proletarian future.

44. *Ibid.*, p. 85. Gorky's speech at the session of the Presidium of the Union of Soviet Writers on March 7, 1936.

45. Lavretsky, *Esteticheskie vzglyady russkikh pisateley,* pp. 293, 301.

46. Cf. *Mezh. svyazi russkoy lit.*, p. 349

47. Cf. Weil, *Gorky,* p. 127, and Lavretsky, *Esteticheskie vzglyady russkikh pisateley,* p. 302.

48. Gorky, *Sobr. soch.*, XXVII, 310. From his Marxist point of view, Gorky recognized, despite all differences, "the typological unity of the 'superfluous man' in the West and in Russia." Lavretsky, *Esteticheskie vzglyady russkikh pisateley,* p. 299.

49. Cf. Weil, *Gorky,* p. 103

50. Ludwig, *Maxim Gorki,* p. 200.

51. N. Ludwig extols *The Mother* as an "imperishable literary Monument," *ibid.*, p. 133. More in keeping with the facts seems the verdict of Setschkareff, "insipid and boring". *Geschichte der russischen Literatur,* p. 136.

52. Cf. Weil: "I do not consider it a terrible denigration of Gorky to assert that he had neither the genius nor the artistic independence of a Tolstoy or a Dostoevsky," *Gorky,* p. 20. Setschkareff is even sterner: "His [Gorky's] novels are . . . a fiasco . . . Gorky's dramas are feeble imitations of Chekhov completely lacking the inner dynamism of his model." *Geschichte der russischen Literatur,* p. 136.

53. Ludwig, *Maxim Gorki,* p. 245. The quotation refers specifically to the tetralogy *Klim Samgin* (1925–36).

54. *Ibid.*, p. 286. For the reception of Gorky in the two parts of Germany see Ilse Idzikowski, "Maxim Gorki in der DDR und in Westdeutschland," *Kunst und Literatur* XVI (1968), 3–18. Cf. also *Maxim Gorki in Deutschland, Bibliographie 1899 bis 1965,* ed. E. Czikowsky, I. Idzikowski, and G. Schwarz (Berlin, 1968).

CHAPTER 3: BLOK

1. *Pisma Aleksandra Bloka k rodnym,* ed. M. A. Beketova (Leningrad, 1927), p. 149. The letter is written in German and dated September 13, 1905. Herzen also called the German poet "my old teacher Schiller." Cf. *Poln.sobr. soch. i pisem* (Petersburg, 1919–25), XXI, 486.

2. But cf. V. Santoli, who sees in Heine a "neobaroque poet." *Fra Germania e Italia* (Firenze, 1962), p. 71.

3. Cf. Robertson: "It was no vainglorious boast when he [Heine] called himself 'a soldier in the liberation War of Humanity.' " *A History of German Literature* (New York, n. d.), p. 503. However, Emil Ermatinger holds a different opinion. Defining Heine as a "Forciertes Talent," he emphasizes: "Aber die Freiheit, für die er kämpfte, war im Grunde nur seine eigene." *Deutsche Dichter* (Bonn, 1948), II, 334.

4. Cf. F. Martini, *Deutsche Literaturgeschichte* (Stuttgart, 1952), p. 268.

5. Aleksandr Blok, *Sochinenia* (Moskva, 1955), II, 307. N.B.: All translations are mine.

6. Blok took his idea of the "spirit of music" from Nietzsche's *Die Geburt der Tragödie.* "Yet Blok's 'spirit of music,' although conceived as the Dionysian force of vital change, bringing chaos in order to create a new cosmos, is understood by the poet in a sense very different from Nietzsche's." R. Poggioli, *The Poets of Russia* (Cambridge, Mass., 1960), p. 188. Cf. also R. M. Longyear, *Schiller and Music* (Chapel Hill, 1966).

7. Cf. V. Ivanov, *Po zvezdam* (Moskva, 1905), p. 85.

8. Cf. Tieck's "Farbenhören" and "Liebe denkt in süssen Tönen." Verlaine ("De la musique avant toute chose"), Rimbaud, and Baudelaire had a strong influence on the Symbolist movement in Russia. See G. Donchin, *The Influence of French Symbolism on Russian Poetry* ('s-Gravenhage, 1958), and R. D. Kluge, *Westeuropa und Russland im Weltbild Aleksandr Bloks* (München, 1967).

9. "Using . . . the favorite terms of that German thinker [Spengler], although in the opposite sense, Blok claims that modern humanism had built a "culture" based on individualism, but that, by its inability to understand the collective, unconscious will of the masses, it had failed to build a real "civilization." Poggioli, *The Poets of Russia,* p. 189.

10. Blok, *Soch.*, II, 732. Blok refers here to the performance of *Don Carlos,* which was "the great event of the theatre season."

11. Aleksandr Blok, *Sobranie sochineniy* (Leningrad, 1936), XII, 185. Almost half a century later, *Don Carlos* became a similar triumphal success at the National Theatre in Warsaw. The historic line spoken by Posa ("Give us freedom of thought") met with resounding applause by a crowd of uniformed soldiers. The play had been running for months with tremendous success. *The New York Times* (July 23, 1963). Certainly a thought-provoking parallel to the performances in revolutionary Petrograd.

12. Blok, *Sobr. soch,* XII, 187.

13. Blok, *Sobr. soch.*, XII, 202–203. Under the spell of Schiller's *Don Carlos,* Herzen and Ogarev took a similar "solemn oath to struggle for the welfare of mankind." Cf. Herzen, *Poln. sobr. soch. i pisem,* XII, 73–74.

14. Blok, *Sobr. soch.*, XII, 210. Blok's optimism and aestheticism look very much like Schiller's, but note that religion and philosophy apparently are not necessary to arrive at an understanding of the "ultimate purpose of life."

15. Blok's considerations resemble Tonio's reflections on the unhappiness of the King. Cf. Thomas Mann, *Tonio Kröger* (Chapter I).

16. Perhaps this was an allusion to the childlike faith of some revolutionaries who firmly believed that it was possible "to renew the earth with one stroke of the pen." Blok did not share this belief any longer. Blok, *Sobr. soch.*, XII, 211.

17. Blok, *Sobr. soch.*, XII, 212. Blok's Posa image is over-idealized. He did not see Posa's ambiguity, his double-crossing with relation to both the King and Don Carlos. Cf. A. von Gronicka, "Friedrich Schiller's Marquis Posa," *Germanic Review,* XXVI (Oct. 1951), 196–214.

18. Perhaps Blok would never have made common cause with the Communists if Maxim Gorky had not convinced him of the desirability and inevitability of a radical break with the past.

19. Strange to say, such an interpretation involuntarily recalls Gottsched's *Versuch einer kritischen Dichtkunst für die Deutschen:* "Die ganze Fabel [of a drama] hat nur eine Hauptabsicht, nämlich einen moralischen Satz."

20. Cf. *Mezhdunarodnye svyazi russkoy literatury,* ed. M. P. Alekseyev (Moskva, 1963), p. 349: "During those years [following the October revolution], M. Gorky, A. Blok, A.V. Lunacharsky, and others were fighting for a heroic theatre the repertoire of which was based on tragedy and melodrama."

21. Blok, *Sobr. soch.*, XII, 213.

22. Blok, *Sobr. soch.*, XII, 215.

23. Blok, *Sobr. soch.*, XII, 213. Regarding the style of Blok's "Speeches" see V. Orlov, *Aleksandr Blok* (Moskva, 1956), p. 251.

24. Blok, *Sobr. soch.*, XII, 223. For details regarding this "return to romanticism," to Sophocles, Shakespeare, and Schiller, cf. Marc Slonim, *Russian Theater* (Cleveland & New York, 1961), p. 282.

25. Cf. *A. Blok i A. Bely—Perepiska,* ed. V. N. Orlov (Moskva, 1940), p. xi. For Blok's debt to V. Solovyov see F. D. Reeve, *Aleksandr Blok* (New York, 1962), pp. 30, 44, 236.

26. Blok, *Soch.*, II, 308. Cf. Demtschenko and Genin: "Die Aufführungen von Schillers Trauerspielen in Petrograd während der Jahre der Revolution und des Bürgerkriegs sind eines der interessantesten und dabei am wenigsten erforschten Kapitel in der Geschichte der Erschliessung des Schillerschen Erbes in Russland. In dieser Epoche traten die charakteristischen Züge der Schillerschen Dramen, ihr heroisches Pathos, ihre politisch-agitatorische Wirkung und Schärfe, ihre Fähigkeit, die Massen zu packen und zu begeistern, besonders deutlich und eindrucksvoll in Erscheinung." "Schiller auf den Bühnen des revolutionären Petrograd," *Sinn und Form,* XI (Berlin, 1959), 927.

27. Cf. Reeve: "It [the Christ-symbol in *The Twelve*] carries everything except the notion of ultimate freedom. This is the basic failure of the poem. . . ." *Aleksandr Blok,* p. 212. Cf. also Sophie Laffitte: "Pourquoi Blok, de 1918 à 1921, fut-il incapable d'écrire des vers? Pourquoi était-il déjà mort trois ans avant sa mort corporelle? A cause du choc qui se produisit au fond de son être lorsque la vraie Révolution contraignit Blok à confronter avec la réalité l'espoir irréel, insensé qu'il portait en lui." *Alexandre Blok* (Paris, 1958), pp. 81–82. But Poggioli concedes that "technically speaking, *The Twelve* is one of Blok's most perfect and mature works." *The Poets of Russia,* p. 205. Incidentally, as for the "fusion of politics and art," a comparison between Blok and Bert Brecht might be very fruitful.

28. Blok, *Sobr. soch.*, XII, 211. Lenin was inclined to "brand all the religious- or mystical-minded symbolists as 'enemies of the people and reactionaries' but it was the symbolists . . . who supported the Revolution in Theatrical Sections or in Literary Conferences. Consequently the continuation of symbolism in poetry, prose, and theater had to be tolerated." Slonim, *Russian Theater,* p. 231.

CHAPTER 4: BOTKIN

1. Ch. Vetrinsky, "V.P. Botkin," *Novoye Slovo,* XII (St. Petersburg, 1894), 40. For details about Stankevich and his circle see "At the Roots of Russian Westernism," *Slavic and East European Studies,* VI (Montreal, 1961), 158–76. All translations are mine.

2. A. Fet, *Moi vospominania* (Moskva, 1890), I, 402–3.

3. Vetrinsky, "V. P. Botkin", p. 46. The Stankevich circle had an antecedent, it "continued the tradition of Prince Odoevski's Philosophical Society of the Twenties." H. Bowman, *V. Belinski* (Cambridge, Mass., 1954), p. 40—When in Paris (1835), Botkin visited Victor Hugo who gave him his autograph with the motto *"Qui sperat vivit."* Cf. A. Zviguilsky, "V.P. Botkin chez Victor Hugo," *Revue de Litterature Comparée,* XXXIX (Paris, June 1965), 290.

4. V. Lazursky, "V.P. Botkin," *Artist,* XLIII (Moskva, 1894), 92. Belinsky borrowed from Botkin also the idea of the advantages of capitalism on Russian soil. Botkin was the first in Russia to voice this idea under the influence of Marx and Lorenz von Stein. Cf. P.N. Sakulin, *Russkaya literatura i sotsializm* (Moskva, 1922), p. 205. As a consequence, the economist and philosopher Pyotr Struve acclaimed Botkin as the "father of Russian Marxism." *Na raznye temy* (St. Petersburg, 1902), p. 106. But the "true" Marxists rejected this claim: "Concerning the clear traces of Marx's influence [on Botkin], they can in our view be best explained by the ascendancy of Annenkov who was the principal champion of this influence. . . ." D. Ryazanov, *Karl Marx i russkie ludi sorokovykh godov* (Petrograd, 1918), p. 97. And even more forcefully: ". . . there is not and cannot be any ideological succession between the "Marxism" of Annenkov and Botkin and contemporary Marxism." *Ibid.,* p. 99.

5. Fet, *Moi vospominania,* p. 431.

6. Vetrinsky, "V. P. Botkin", p. 47. Many years later, in 1855, Botkin remarked with reference to Hegel: "There is certainly something poetic in any profound view. According to my opinion, Hegel is full of poesy." *V.P. Botkin i I. S. Turgenev —Neizdannaya perepiska* (Moskva, 1930), p. 62. However, in a letter of September 29, 1856, he placed Schelling above Hegel: "I think that Schelling gives a far more profound and substantial conception of mythology than does Hegel in his *Religion der Schönheit*—and so on." *Ibid.*, p. 94. For Hegel's impact on Russian thought see D. Chizhevsky, *Gegel v Rossii* (Paris, 1939). For Schelling see W. Setschkareff, *Schellings Einfluss in der Russischen Literatur* (Leipzig, 1939)—Due to his friendship with Bakunin, Botkin was placed under "secret police surveillance" in 1852. Cf. A. Lyaskovsky, *Martirolog russkikh pisateley* (Berlin, 1956), p. 318. Cf. also "Bakunin," *Monatshefte,* LIV (March 1962), 109–16.

7. Lazursky, "V.P. Botkin," p. 95. Botkin did not think much of Shakespeare's early dramatic efforts: "All these first seven youthful plays bear both in form and in content the imprint of the rather vulgar popular taste which reigned on the English stage before Shakespeare." *Sochinenia V. P. Botkina* (St. Petersburg, 1890), II, 157–58, hereafter abridged to *Soch.* According to Botkin, *Henry VI* was the first

play in which Shakespeare "poured out all his immense power." *Hamlet, Lear, Othello,* and *Macbeth* are eulogized as his "most profound and all-embracing tragedies of truly cosmic dimensions." *Soch.*, II, 162. Botkin sums up as follows: "Each drama by Shakespeare comprises a universe which is complete in itself. It lives by its own idea anchored in its depths. Thus it carries its justification and proof in itself and not in the personality and circumstances of the poet." *Soch.*, II, 224.

8. N. Izmaylov, "Pisma V. P. Botkina," *Literaturnaya Mysl,* II (Petrograd, 1923), 160. Belinsky was well aware of this "gift" when he urged Botkin to write a detailed *Life of Schiller:* "It would be a great work and you could carry it off excellently. And what a boon that would be for our society!" Belinsky, *Pisma* (St. Petersburg, 1914), II, 221. Botkin never wrote the proposed "great work". As a matter of fact, more than a hundred years passed until the first biography of the German poet was published on Russian soil: Frants P. Schiller, *Fridrikh Schiller* (Moskva, 1955). Though a landmark in Russian Schiller scholarship, it is not on a par with comparable Western Schiller biographies. L. Lozinskaya's *Schiller* (Moskva, 1960), is—in the author's words—"the first popular biography of the poet written by a Soviet author."

9. Lazursky, "V.P. Botkin," p. 95. As for Gutzkow's *Letters from Paris,* Belinsky agreed with Botkin that the German writer was "narrow-minded, abstract, and ignorant of the spirit of the times." Cf. Belinsky, *Poln. sobr. soch.* (Moskva, 1956), XII, 152. Cf. also *Mezhdunarodnye svyazi russkoy literatury* (Moskva, 1963), p. 347.

10. "Pisma V. G. Belinskogo i V.P. Botkina k A. A. Krayevskomu," *Otchet Imperatorskoy Publichnoy Biblioteki za 1889 g.* (St. Petersburg, 1893), Prilozhenia, p. 69.

11. Botkin, *Soch.*, II, 270.

12. *Ibid.*, p. 267. Regarding Schiller's "consciousness of history," it should be kept in mind that his dramas were initially written under the impact of his own personal experiences. His interest in history begins only with *Don Carlos,* and the "consciousness of history" which he develops is tied up with his poetic interest in certain historical figures (King Philip, Wallenstein, Maria Stuart, etc.). Cf. also Schiller's letter to Körner, which reveals a very concrete material interest: "Ich sehe nicht ein, warum ich nicht, wenn ich ernstlich will, der erste Geschichtsschreiber in Deutschland werden kann: und dem ersten müssen sich doch auf jeden Fall Aussichten eröffnen." Letter of November 26, 1790.—Botkin's interest in the theatre remained alive throughout the following years. In 1855, for instance, he eagerly collaborated with Grigorovich, Druzhinin, and I. S. Turgenev in the writing and production of a comedy in which the latter played a significant part. Cf. B.V. Varneke, *History of the Russian Theatre* (New York, 1951), p. 400.

13. Botkin, *Soch.*, II, 277

14. *Ibid.*, p. 278. Botkin's view contrasts with the interpretation of a German critic who holds that it was Schiller's aim to express in "Ritter Toggenburg" "die Idee der unüberwindlichen, durch die Unmöglichkeit der Erfüllung nur vertieften, verklärten Liebe." *Schillers Sämtliche Werke,* Säkular-Ausgabe, I, 311

(notes). As for "Der Handschuh," Schiller simply regarded it "ein kleines Nachstück zum 'Taucher' " (letter to Goethe of June 18, 1797). In this case, the odds apparently are against Botkin.

15. Botkin, *Soch,* II, 279.

16. "Von den sämtlichen Gedichten Rückerts werden die sieben magern die sieben fetten fressen, und nichts wird übrig bleiben." Grillparzer, *Sämtliche Werke,* ed. W. Eichner (Berlin, n.d.), XVI, 55. "Viel Minderwertiges erstickt bei ihm [Rückert] die echten lyrischen Gebilde. . . ." F. Martini, *Deutsche Literaturgeschichte* (Stuttgart, 1952), p. 339. "Träte man . . . an Gedichte wie die von Rückert heran, so könnte man nur die Abwesenheit alles dessen feststellen, was ein Gedicht zum Gedicht machen und als Gedicht ausmachen soll." J. Pfeiffer, *Die deutsche Lyrik,* ed. B. von Wiese (Düsseldorf, 1959), II, 116.

17. Vetrinsky, "V.P. Botkin", p. 70.

18. Lazursky, "V.P. Botkin," p. 94. In his *Letters on Spain* Botkin stressed the importance of the "economic factor" and defended the West European bourgeoisie against the attacks of the Slavophiles and Herzen. He also gave high praise to the Spanish national character and to the genius of the Spanish people. For this reason, Botkin's *Letters on Spain* has been disparaged by Soviet criticism as an expression of "kowtowing before the bourgeois culture of Western Europe." Cf. *Bolshaya Sovetskaya Entsiklopedia* (Moskva, 1950), V, 642. Cf. also Ryazanov, *Karl Marx i russkie ludi sorokovykh godov,* p. 95.

19. Botkin, *Soch.*, II, 375.

20. Izmaylov, "Pisma V. P. Botkina," pp. 159–60.

21. *Ibid.*, p. 160. In this respect, Botkin resembles his friend Stankevich who often rejected romanticism on logical grounds while accepting it on the grounds of empathy. Cf. Bowman, *V. Belinski,* p. 43 Cf. also V. Zenkovsky, *A History of Russian Philosophy* (New York, 1953), I, 240.

22. Fet, *Moi vospominania,* I, 401.

23. *Ibid.*, p. 402.

24. *Ibid.*

25. *Ibid.* The last lines of Botkin's letter seem to invalidate Soviet charges that "Botkin joined hands with Katkov, the advocate of 'ruthless power' (and Capitalism). His former [liberal] dreams evaporated into thin air without leaving a trace." *Bolshaya Sovetskaya Entsiklopedia* (Moskva, 1927), VII, 251.

26. Fet, *Moi vospominania,* 402.

27. *Ibid.*, p. 403.

28. Lazursky, "*V. P. Botkin,*" p. 93.

29. *Ibid.*, p. 94. This Beethoven concert took place in February, 1866.

30. *Ibid.*. p. 97. Botkin's statement must not be taken literally. In reality, he continued to "care" for many things. "It would be a mistake to think that Botkin absolutely isolated himself from life . . . his interest in social and political problems did not flag." Sakulin, *Russkaya literatura i sotsializm,* p. 207. Nor did his interest in literature and philosophy completely die. Toward the end of his life, "he [Botkin] made the doctrines of two great contemporary thinkers—Carlyle

and Schopenhauer—the basis of his philosophical contemplations." P.V. Annenkov, *Literaturnye vospominania* (Moskva, 1960), p. 331. In particular, Botkin took from Carlyle the idea that there was a redemptive force in hero-worship and deference to authority. Schopenhauer, on the other hand, impressed him with his disdain of the masses and of objectless philosophizing.

31. Vetrinsky, "*V. P. Botkin,*" p. 105. "Frustration" is an important phenomenon in Russian life and letters. The figure of the "superfluous man" persisted even in Soviet literature and disappeared only with the introduction of the theory of Socialist Realism in the middle thirties. Also Botkin's friend Stankevich felt himself a "superfluous man" toward the end of his short life. Cf. *Stankevich—Perepiska* (Moskva, 1914), p. 650.

32. *Bolshaya Sovetskaya Entsiklopedia* (Moskva, 1950), V, 642. Soviet criticism contrasts with the high esteem in which Botkin was held by his contemporaries. Cp., for instance, L. Tolstoy's saying that Botkin was "the most exquisite and the wisest of his friends" and, indeed, "his most indispensable conversation partner." Cf. "Lettres inédites de L. Tolstoi a Botkine," *Les oeuvres libres* (Paris, 1926), p. 5 ff.

33. *Bolshaya Sovetskaya Entsiklopedia* (1950), V. 642. After 1860, Botkin broke with Chernyshevsky, Herzen, and Nekrasov because "the violent outbursts of the Young Russians of the sixties repelled and frightened him." Sakulin, *Russkaya lit. i sotsializm,* p. 210. Botkin was equally frightened by the violence of the Polish revolution of 1863. But his indignation at the pro-Polish position of the radicals and his denunciation of *Kolokol* and *Sovremennik* were "the voice of a dying old man—and it would hardly seem right to attach too much importance to similar moods of Botkin and quite unfair to draw his general portrait under this aspect." Sakulin, *Russkaya literatura i sotsializm,* p. 211. As a matter of fact, Botkin became a champion of gradual and prudent progress during the last years of his life. In this respect, he may be compared with Schiller, who began as an advocate of revolution and ended as a champion of the unhurried aesthetic education of humanity.

34. *Bolshaya Sovetskaya Entsiklopedia* (1927), VII, 251. Hence the inescapable corollary that a critical edition of Botkin's correspondence has been overdue for almost half a century. It may fall to the lot of Western literary scholarship to answer the challenge.

CHAPTER 5: GRANOVSKY

1. Ivan Tkhorzhevsky, *Russkaya literatura* (Paris, 1950), p. 218. Cf. also Adolf Stender-Petersen: "Als der junge geniale Professor T. N. Granovskij . . . im Herbstsemester 1843 seine öffentlichen Universitätsvorlesungen über die Geschichte des europäischen Mittelalters hielt und diese mit grosser Begeisterung aufgenommen wurden, entstand im slavophilen Lager Unruhe, und der tüchtige, jedoch weniger geniale Professor S. P. Ševyr'ov (1806–64) beeilte sich, im Jahre darauf öffentliche Vorlesungen über russische Literatur zu halten, die dann eine fast ebenso imposante Hörerschar anzogen wie die seines jüngeren Kollegen."

Geschichte der Russischen Literatur (München, 1957), II, 199.

2. S. A. Asinovskaya, *Iz istorii peredovykh idei v russkoy medievistike* (Moskva, 1955), p. 23. Asinovskaya does not mention Goethe, who had a strong impact on Granovsky. Cf. I. S. Turgenev, "Dva slova o Granovskom": "I made his acquaintance in 1835 in Petersburg at the university. . . . He even wrote verses at that time . . . and I vaguely remember a fragment from a drama *Faust* which he read to me one dark winter night. In this fragment Faust was . . . hovering high in the air in a glass box together with Mephistopheles. Viewing the outspread earth, rivers, woods, fields, and human dwellings, Faust delivered a monologue full of sad contemplation which seemed very beautiful to me at that time. . . . Mephistopheles was silent. To be sure, even now I cannot imagine what words Granovsky could have put into the mouth of the devil. . . . Irony, especially caustic and merciless irony, was foreign to his pure soul." *Izbrannye sochinenia T. N. Granovskogo,* ed. V. A. Sokolov, (Moskva, 1905), p. xii-xiii.

3. N. Sidorov, "T. N. Granovsky," *Besedy* (Moskva, 1915), p. 2. The impact of Western thought on Granovsky was very great, indeed: "Granovsky stayed abroad, mainly in Berlin, for three years. All his moral, philosophical, scientific, and historical views arose and took shape during that time." Ch. Vetrinsky, *Gumanist 40-kh godov* (Moskva, 1905), p. 8. Cf. also D. M. Levshin, *N. Granovsky* (St. Petersburg, 1901), p. 132 ff.

4. *T. N. Granovsky i yego perepiska* (Moskva, 1897), II, 390. Hereafter abridged to *Perepiska.* Ch. Vetrinsky remarks in this connection: "These references to Schiller are interesting because they give an idea of Granovsky's personality: Schiller's humane and sublime, though at times nebulous, idealism was in perfect accord with Granovsky's fanciful, youthful romanticism and also with the influence which Stankevich began to exercise upon him." *T. N. Granovsky i yego vremya* (St. Petersburg, 1905), p. 31. Other important influences were Tacitus and Shakespeare: "What a great soul [Tacitus]! Besides Shakespeare, no one has been able to give me [Granovsky] a greater enjoyment." *Ibid.*, p. 32.

5. *Perepiska,* II, 62–63. S. A. Asinovskaya emphasizes the socio-political aspect of this influence: "Pushkin's poetry of freedom and the protest against despotism resounding in the works of his beloved Shakespeare and Schiller . . . could not fail to have a profound effect on the molding of young Granovsky's intellect." *Lektsii T. N. Granovskogo po istorii srednevekovya* (Moskva, 1961), p. 4. It appears, however, that Granovsky experienced the works of these "beloved poets" in a very personal and completely unpolitical way at that time. N. B. Granovsky sometimes wrote in French.

6. *Perepiska,* II, 392. Schiller's drama was a source of inspiration also to Smetana who created a symphonic poem entitled *Wallensteins Lager.*

7. Cp. André von Gronicka, "Friedrich Schiller's Marquis Posa," *Germanic Review,* XXVI (Oct. 1951), 196–214.

8. *Perepiska,* II, 346.

9. N. P. Ogarev, *Izbrannye sotsialno-politicheskie i filosofskie proizvedenia* (Moskva, 1952), II, 590.

10. *Perepiska,* II, 349.

11. *Perepiska,* II, 355–56. It is interesting to note that at that time (1838) Stankevich earnestly considered the possibility of publishing an almanac on the model of the "Xenien" together with his friend Granovsky. Cf. *N. V. Stankevich-Perepiska* (Moskva, 1914), p. 468.

12. *Perepiska,* I, 108. As for Belinsky's hostility to Schiller, cf. V. G. Belinsky, *Pisma* (St. Petersburg, 1914), I, 346–47.

13. *Perepiska,* I, 109.

14. *Perepiska,* II, 364. Belinsky's low esteem of *Wallenstein* is indicative rather of fanaticism than of critical acumen. Many will agree with Janko Lavrin that "*Boris Godunov* is certainly less brilliant with regard to its 'poetic side' than Schiller's *Demetrius,* for example." *Pushkin* (London, 1947), p. 151.

15. *Perepiska,* II, 378. M. N. Zagoskin (1789–1852) was a writer of nationalistic historical novels in the manner of Scott. By placing the German poet "on a level with Zagoskin," Belinsky openly showed that he held Schiller in contempt at that time (1840).

16. *Perepiska,* II, 190. Granovsky here refers to the biography by Gustav B. Schwab, *Schillers Leben* (Stuttgart, 1840). Granovsky's view that Schiller was "plus qu'un grand poète" tallies with the findings of recent Schiller scholarship. Cf., for instance, W. Witte: "What strikes one again and again in Schiller's writings . . . is their relevance to the events and problems, political, social, and spiritual, of our own age." *Schiller-Bicentenary Lectures,* ed. F. Norman (London, 1960), p. 149.

17. *Perepiska,* II, 198. Letter of June 24, 1841.

18. In the past, the prejudice prevailed that Schiller's historical writings were "brilliant in form but uncritical." Modern historians hold a different opinion. Cf. Golo Mann, "Schiller als Geschichtsschreiber": "Schiller liess bei dem Gebrauch der historischen Quellen . . . seine kritische Intelligenz walten." *Geschichte und Geschichten* (Frankfurt, 1961), p. 69. Cf. also Theodor Schieder: "Wir sind damit auf einem überraschend hohen Gipfel der Einschätzung von Schillers historiographischer Leistung angelangt. . . ." *Begegnungen mit der Geschichte* (Göttingen, 1962), p. 58.

19. Overwhelmed by doubts, "Granovsky turned to Hegel to calm and reconcile these doubts." At times, however, he took pride in being a doubter: "Doubt we can, doubt we must—this is one of man's sublime rights." Cf. Vetrinsky, *Gumanist 40-kh godov,* p. 9. In addition to Hegel, Granovsky read also Gibbon, Guizot, and Thierry. Of all the American authors "Granovsky especially loved Emerson." *Perepiska,* I, 267.

20. *Sochinenia T. N. Granovskogo* (Moskva, 1900), p. 28–29.

21. It seems plausible that Schiller's *Don Carlos* contributed to the shaping of Granovsky's concept of tolerance and brotherly love.

22. The last clause is reminiscent of Goethe's *Faust:* "Ein Teil von jener Kraft, /Die stets das Böse will und stets das Gute schafft."

23. Cf. *Perepiska,* I, 267.

24. *Ibid.*

25. A. I. Gertsen, *Polnoye sobranie sochineniy i pisem,* ed. M. K. Lemke (St. Petersburg, 1919–25), XIII, 117.

26. N. V. Minayeva, *Granovsky v Moskve* (Moskva, 1963).

27. *Bolshaya Sovetskaya Entsiklopedia,* XII (1952), 447.

28. *Ibid.*

29. *Ibid.*, p. 448.

CHAPTER 6: PUSHKIN

1. Cf. Otto P. Peterson, *Schiller in Russland* (New York, 1934); Edmund Kostka, *Schiller in Russian Literature* (Philadelphia, 1965); Hans-Bernd Harder, *Schiller in Russland* (Bad Homburg, 1969).

2. D. Čyževskyj, "Schiller und die Brüder Karamasow," *Zeitschrift für Slawische Philologie* VI (Leipzig, 1929), 3.

3. There was a widespread belief that Pushkin "did not like at all German literature" and that "he did not even try to become acquainted with it." *Sochinenia A. S. Pushkina,* ed. P. O. Morozov (St. Petersburg, 1887), I, 118.

4. F. Dostoyevsky, *Polnoye sobranie sochineniy* (St. Petersburg, 1883–1904), I, 15–16.

5. *Schiller,* ed. S. A. Vengerov (St. Petersburg, 1900), I, i.

6. J. Thomas Shaw, "Recent Soviet Scholarly Books on Puškin," *Slavic and East European Journal,* X (Spring 1966), 84.

7. Cf. Rudolf Fischer, "Schiller und Puschkin," *Wissenschaftliche Zeitschrift der Karl Marx-Universität Leipzig,* IX (Leipzig, 1959–60), 73–76.

8. Henri Troyat, *Pushkin* (New York, 1950), pp. 44, 53.

9. Cf. *Pushkin,* ed. S. A. Vengerov (St. Petersburg, 1907–15), I, 158; *Sochinenia M. V. Milonova,* ed. A. Smirdin (St. Petersburg, 1849), pp. 70–74: "Iz 'Mat' ubiytsa' Schillera" ("From 'The Infanticide' by Schiller").

10. Cf. *Pushkin i yego sovremenniki* (St. Petersburg, 1913), pp. 250–54. To be sure, "social criticism" is certainly implied in Schiller's poem and Benno von Wiese is basically right when he says: "Soziale Kritik des Sturm und Drang, insbesondere im Stile Schubarts, äussert sich in den Cedichten 'Die Kindsmörderin,' 'Die schlimmen Monarchen.' " *Friedrich Schiller* (Stuttgart, 1963), p. 132.

11. Cf. *Soch. Pushkina,* ed. Morozov, I, 118; Yury Veselovsky, "Schiller kak vdokhnovitel russkikh pisateley," *Russkaya Mysl,* II (Moskva, 1906), 5.

12. Cf. G. D. Vladimirsky, "Pushkin-perevodchik," *Pushkin,* IV–V (Moskva-Leningrad, 1939), 318. For G. N. Gennady see *Sochinenia i pisma Pushkina,* ed. P. O. Morozov (St. Petersburg, 1903), I, 471 (notes).

13. *Sochinenia Pushkina,* ed. Leonid Maykov (St. Petersburg, 1900–29), I, 255. Under tragic circumstances and, as it were, under the auspices of Schiller, Pushkin and Küchelbecker met again on October 15, 1827, while the latter was being transported to his place of exile in Siberia: "At the next station I [Pushkin] found *The Visionary* by Schiller. But I hardly managed to read the first few pages when suddenly four vehicles arrived accompanied by a gendarme. . . ." Pushkin, *Polnoye*

sobranie sochineniy (Ak. Nauk SSSR, 1937–49), XII, 307. Hereafter abridged to *PSS*.

14. V. G. Belinsky, *Polnoye sobranie sochineniy* (Moskva, 1953–59), VII, 287. Without realizing it, Belinsky pointed out a Schiller parallel in his fifth article on Pushkin: "Pushkin faithfully depicted lands he had never seen." One may call to mind Schiller's *Wilhelm Tell* and, in the case of Pushkin, his magnificent fragment *Egyptian Nights*.

15. *Soch. Pushkina* (1900–29), I, 259.

16. Troyat, *Pushkin*, p. 77.

17. Cf. V. A. Zhukovsky, *Stikhotvorenia* (Leningrad, 1956), pp. 413–17. V. Cheshikhin is definitely wrong when he says that "all of Zhukovsky's imitations of Schiller's lyric poetry are weak." *Zhukovsky kak perevodchik Schillera* (Riga, 1895), p. 51. See also M. Ehrhard, *Joukovski et le pré-romantisme russe* (Paris, 1938), and M. Volm, *W. A. Zhukovskij als Übersetzer* (Ann Arbor, Michigan, 1945).

18. Very close to Schiller are also Pushkin's poems "To Delvig" (1817), "I don't regret the years of bygone spring" (1820), "You're right, my friend" (1821), and "War" (1821). All these verses reflect in form, mood, and content the basic themes of Schiller's poetry, especially the themes of "Die Ideale": sorrow about the passing of youth, love, and poetic inspiration, the conception of life as a pilgrimage, lamentation over the collapse of juvenile dreams and aspirations, etc. For details see Z. Rozova, "Pushkin i 'Idealy' Schillera," *Slavia*, XIV (Prague, 1936–37), 384–88.

19. Pushkin, *PSS*, II, 131. Many years later, in 1833, Pushkin participated in concocting a merry trifle about "The cook or historian Miller, /The German poet Schiller, /And Pinetti, the famous Taschenspieler." *Ibid.*, III[1], 488.

20. Troyat, *Pushkin*, p. 85. Pushkin's French-oriented childhood education was doubtless an important factor in his attitude toward the German language. Lermontov, on the other hand, "enjoyed an important advantage in his appreciation of German literature . . . by having been raised in a singularly Germanophile home." André von Gronicka, "Lermontov's Debt to Goethe," *Revue de Littérature Comparée*, XL (Winter, 1966), 568. Regarding his study of the German language, Pushkin himself once confessed to Ksenofont Polevoy: "It's only with German that I cannot cope. I master it and again forget everything: to be sure, this happened to me more than once." *Rukoyu Pushkina*, ed. M. A. Pavlovsky (Moskva-Leningrad, 1935), p. 23.

21. B. V. Varneke, *History of the Russian Theatre* (New York, 1951), p. 211.

22. B. Tomashevsky, *Pushkin* (Moskva-Leningrad, 1956), I, 269.

23. Pushkin, *PSS*, XI, 10. Pushkin may have seen Semyonova also in *King Lear*, *Oedipus*, *Tancred*, *Antigone*, *Mérope*, and *Iphigenia*. Cf. Tomashevsky, *Pushkin*, I, 269.

24. Cf. *Ostafyevsky Arkhiv Knyazey Vyazemskikh* (St. Petersburg, 1899), II[1], 327. On May 31, 1823, Prince Vyazemsky wrote to A. I. Turgenev: "I offer my thanks to him [Pushkin] because he does not deprive us poor prisoners of the hope of swimming even with chains on our feet."

25. Cf. Tomashevsky, *Pushkin*, I, 458.

26. Belinsky, *Polnoye sobranie sochineniy*, VII, 384.

27. *Pushkin-kritik*, ed. N. V. Bogoslovsky (Moskva, 1950), p. 25. Pushkin made

this reference to Schiller in connection with the subject matter of his "The Prisoner in the Caucasus." He probably thought of the analogy between the flaming love of the Circassian girl for the prisoner who had grown cold and Pygmalion's ardent infatuation with the statue. Cf. Rozova, "Pushkin i 'Idealy' Schillera," p. 396.

28. Pushkin, *PSS,* XIII 45. Letter of September 4, 1822. Unrhymed pentameters on the stage excited and worried not only Pushkin but also Karamzin who apprehensively exclaimed: "I don't know how our actors will perform it [Schiller's *Maid of Orleans*]: this is a novel in dialogue form and not a drama." Pushkin, *PSS,* VII, 371. Evidently, Karamzin was afraid of the innovation as such whereas Pushkin's words express a fear that the innovation might prove a failure.

29. *Soch. Pushkina* (1900–29), IX, 929 (notes). Italics Pushkin's. N. B. Pushkin often wrote in French or interspersed his letters with French words.

30. Pushkin, *PSS,* XIII, 163. Letter of April 22, 1825.

31. *Pushkin-Pisma,* ed. B. L. Modzalevsky (Moskva-Leningrad, 1926) I, 431 (notes).

32. Troyat, *Pushkin,* p. 229.

33. *Ibid.,* p. 232. Perhaps Pushkin learned his "rules" from Schiller's treatise "Über die tragische Kunst" (1790). But the outcome of these theoretical studies, *Boris Godunov,* does not quite measure up to the standard of a "masterpiece of world literature" (Troyat, p. 232). Cf. Janko Lavrin: "*Boris Godunov* is certainly less brilliant with regard to its 'poetic side' than Schiller's *Demetrius,* for example." *Pushkin and Russian Literature* (London, 1947), p. 151.

34. Troyat, *Pushkin,* p. 231. At this time, Pushkin placed Shakespeare sky-high above Byron whom he had admired three or four years earlier. According to Shevyrev, "Pushkin did not read Shakespeare (as well as Goethe and Schiller) in the original but in an old French translation revised by Guizot. Nonetheless, since he was a genius he understood him perfectly." *Pushkin i yego sovremenniki,* p. 71.

35. Cf. Pushkin, *PSS,* VII, 502 (notes).

36. The usurper theme is not uncommon in European literature. Apart from Schiller and Pushkin, it was elaborated by Lope de Vega, Richard Cumberland, G. Alexander, Bodenstedt, Kotzebue, Lenz, Hebbel, and others.

37. P. Kropotkin, *Ideals and Realities in Russian Literature* (New York, 1925), p. 40. Despite his high praise for *Yevgeny Onegin,* Kropotkin continues: "But, apart from his very latest productions in the dramatic style, there is in whatever Pushkin wrote none of the depth and elevation of ideas which characterized Goethe and Schiller, Shelley, Byron, and Browning, Victor Hugo and Barbier." *Ibid.* In sharp contrast to Kropotkin's praise stands the stricture by the poet N. M. Yazykov: "I did not like *Onegin* at all: I think this work is Pushkin's worst. . . . We are pygmies in comparison with the giants Goethe and Schiller. . . ." *Russkie pisateli 19 veka o Pushkine,* ed. A. S. Dolinin (Leningrad, 1938), pp. 92–93. The attitude of present-day criticism is very different: "Es gibt wohl kaum ein Werk in der Weltliteratur, in dem die objektive Kraft des realistischen Romans so vollkommen mit der Subjektivität der Lyrik und verstehender Ironie vereinigt wäre." V. Setschkareff, *Geschichte der russischen Literatur* (Stuttgart, 1966), p. 83.

38. *Pushkin v mirovoy literature*, Sbornik (Leningrad, 1926), p. 352. It was a fairly comprehensive panorama of German literature that Pushkin could thus obtain ranging from the *Nibelungenlied* over Luther and Lessing to the coryphaei of German romanticism. He certainly took note of the fact that Mme. de Staël characterized Schiller as "a man of rare genius and perfect conscientiousness," and that she found Schiller the more attractive personality in comparison with Goethe.

39. Cf. Rozova, "Pushkin i 'Idealy' Schillera," p. 388.

40. *Pushkin v mirovoy literature*, p. 64. "By candle light he [Lensky] opened Schiller . . ." *Yevgeny Onegin*, VI, 20.

41. Cf. Rozova, "Pushkin i 'Idealy' Schillera," p. 389: "With Lensky, Pushkin buried his youth and his youthful ideals."

42. Cf. Rozova, *ibid.*, p. 391.

43. Troyat, *Pushkin*, p. 272. (Pushkin in his diary notes). At this point, one should keep in mind that Pushkin was not a theoretician. In contrast to Schiller, he never elaborated a definite philosophical *Weltanschauung*. Cf. Sergey fon Shteyn, *Pushkin mistik* (Riga, 1931), p. 58. Noteworthy in this connection that Pushkin knew and valued highly Schiller's historical drama *Fiesko*. Cf. Veselovsky, "Schiller kak vdokhnovitel russkikh pisateley," p. 6.

44. Lavrin, *Pushkin and Russian Literature*, p. 187. Also Goethe's *Götz* and Kleist's *Michael Kohlhaas* served as models for Dubrovsky. Cf. Ettore Lo Gatto *Puškin* (Milano, 1959), p. 508.

45. Cf. Marina Bersano Begey, *Storia della letteratura polacca* (Milano, 1957), p. 144–45.

46. Pushkin, *PSS*, XIV, 170. Letter of June 1, 1831.

47. Pushkin, *PSS*, XIV, 175. Also Pushkin's correspondence to Zhukovsky shows that he was deeply interested in the latter's translations from Schiller. Cp., for instance, Pushkin's letter to Zhukovsky of April 20, 1825: "For goodness' sake, do complete "The Diver." Pushkin, *PSS*, XIII, 167.

48. Pushkin, *PSS*, XIV, 244. Letter of November 28, 1831.

49. Lavrin, *Pushkin and Russian Literature*, p. 181.

50. *Russkie pisateli 19 veka o Pushkine*, p. 115.

51. *Ibid.* Comparable to Lessing in German literature, Pushkin was the first writer in Russian literature who conceived the idea of making literary activity a profession.

52. Pushkin, *PSS*, XII, 69.

53. Troyat, *Pushkin*, p. 474.

54. Aleksandr Blok, *Sochinenia* (Moskva, 1955), II, 354. Speech on the 84th anniversary of Pushkin's death (February 11, 1921).

55. Cf. *Soch. Pushkina*, ed. Morozov (1887), V, 159. Delvig read all the works of Goethe and Schiller in the original with the help of Küchelbecker. Since Pushkin and Küchelbecker were very close friends it is hard to believe that the latter did not extend a similar favor to Aleksandr. We know that Pushkin felt "sacred awe" for the creator of *Faust*. His "Demon" and *Scene from Faust* bear the imprint of Goethe's masterpiece. Cf. A. von Gronicka, *The Russian Image of Goethe* (Philadelphia, 1968), pp. 60–74. Also Pushkin's *Poltava* shows traces of Goethe's

influence. The lines, "Kto pri zvezdakh i pri lune/Tak pozdno yedet na kone," are reminiscent of Goethe's ballad "Erlkönig": "Wer reitet so spät durch Nacht und Wind?/Es ist der Vater mit seinem Kind."

56. Cf. Rozova, "Pushkin i 'Idealy' Schillera," p. 404.

57. Schiller's aesthetic and philosophical views found "an indirect but very distinct echo in the works of such writers as Zhukovsky, Pushkin, and Gogol." A. Gruzinsky, *Literaturnoye ocherki* (Moskva, 1902), p. 43. Of course, this is an inadequate list of names and numerous other Russian writers can be mentioned who fell under the spell of the German poet at one time or another. Thus, Schiller left an imprint on the works of Tyutchev, Turgenev, Chernyshevsky, Dostoyevsky, V. Ivanov, Bely, Blok, Pasternak, and many others.

58. A. von Gronicka, *The Russian Image of Goethe,* p. 68.

59. *Ibid.*, p. 74. This sounds like an underestimation of Goethe's sway over Pushkin. Many other passages in von Gronicka's excellent study convey the idea of a truly significant influence by Goethe on the Russian poet. Cf. Chapter Three, pp. 60–74.

60. Pushkin is an incomparable creator of poetic images. "In this respect, Pushkin is the poet of poets; he is even more spontaneous than Goethe and Schiller because there is far less tendency in him." *Pushkinskaya yubileynaya literatura 1899–1900,* ed. V. Sipovsky (St. Petersburg, 1902), p. 169. Cp. also Setschkareff: "Die eigentliche Domäne Puškins ist die Lyrik." *Geschichte der russischen Literatur,* p. 80. In this connection, it is not without significance that a scholar of the caliber of Vittorio Santoli tends to regard Schiller "rather as a theorist than as a poet." *Storia della letteratura tedesca* (Firenze, 1967), p. 302. Worthy of notice are, furthermore, the apposite observations of Kropotkin: "It is extremely interesting to compare Pushkin with Schiller, in their lyrics. Leaving aside the greatness and the variety of subjects touched upon by Schiller, and comparing only those pieces of poetry in which both poets speak of themselves, one feels at once that Schiller's personality is infinitely superior, in depth of thought and philosophical comprehension of life, to that of the bright, somewhat spoiled and rather superficial child that Pushkin was. But, at the same time, the individuality of Pushkin is more deeply impressed upon his writings than that of Schiller upon his." Kropotkin concludes by affirming: "In his best lyrics Schiller did not find either a better expression of feeling, or a greater variety of expression, than Pushkin did. In that respect the Russian poet decidedly stands by the side of Goethe." Kropotkin, *Ideals and Realities in Russian Literature,* pp. 40–41.

61. J. Thomas Shaw, "Recent Soviet Scholarly Books on Puškin," pp. 81–82. There is, of course, frequent "dialogue" between Soviet scholars and Marxist scholars in the West. Yet its results are precarious, as can be seen in the case of Pushkin's relationship with Schiller. A literary affinity emerges as socio-political solidarity and the two poets appear as comrades in the struggle for a classless society: "Und über Zeit und Raum erhielt Schiller in Puschkin einen Mitstreiter für seine Ziele: vom Sturm und Drang und von den Idealen der Jugend bis zum Wollen des Mannes und bis zum letzten Gefecht." Rudolf Fischer, "Schiller und Puschkin," *Weimarer Beiträge,* III (1960), 611.

Bibliography

INTRODUCTION

Secondary Sources

Brand, Hans Erich. *Kleist und Dostojevskij.* Bonn, 1970.

Chizhevsky, D. *Gegel v Rossii.* Paris, 1939;

———. *Hegel bei den Slaven.* Bad Homburg, 1961.

Durylin, S. "Russkie pisateli u Gete v Veimare." *Literaturnoye Nasledstvo,* IV–VI (Moskva, 1932), 81–504.

Grasshoff, H. *A. D. Kantemir und West-Europa.* Berlin, 1966.

Harder, H. B. *Schiller in Russland.* Bad Homburg, 1969.

Hofman, Alois. *Thomas Mann und die Welt der russischen Literatur.* Berlin, 1967.

Kersten, Gerhard. *Gerhart Hauptmann und Lev Nikolajevič Tolstoj.* Wiesbaden, 1966.

Kopelew, Lew. "Heinrich Bölls Gedichte," *Die Zeit* (July 20, 1971), p. 9.

*For easy reference, bibliographic entries are listed under the chapters in which they occur and grouped as primary and secondary sources. Within this grouping the items are listed alphabetically by author.

———. *Zwei Epochen deutsch-russischer Literaturbeziehungen.* Frankfurt, 1973.

Kostka, Edmund. *Schiller in Russian Literature.* Philadelphia, 1965.

———. Review of Hofman, *Thomas Mann und die Welt der russischen Literatur, Rivista di letterature moderne e comparate,* XXIII (Firenze, Dec. 1970), 314–16.

Krauss, W., ed. *Slawisch-deutsche Wechselseitigkeit in Sprache, Literatur und Kultur.* Berlin, 1968.

Laage, K. E. *Theodor Storm und Iwan Turgenjew.* Heide, 1967.

Lehmann, U. *Der Gottschedkreis und Russland.* Berlin, 1966.

Meier-Graefe, J. *Dostojewski, der Dichter.* Berlin, 1926.

Motylyova, Tamara L. *O mirovom znachenii L. N. Tolstogo.* Moskva, 1957.

Nilsson, Nils Ake. *Ibsen in Russland.* Stockholm, 1958.

Nötzel, K. *Das Leben Dostojewskis.* Leipzig, 1925.

Passage, Charles. *The Russian Hoffmannists.* The Hague, 1963.

Peterson, O. P. *Schiller in Russland.* New York, 1934; vol. II, New York, 1939.

Raab, H. *Die Lyrik Puškins in Deutschland.* Berlin, 1964.

Reber, Natalie. *Studien zum Motiv des Doppelgängers bei Dostojevskij und E. T. A. Hoffman.* Giessen, 1964.

Reissner, E. *Alexander Herzen in Deutschland.* Berlin, 1963.

Schütz, Katharina, *Das Goethebild Turgeniews.* Bern, 1952

Setschkareff, W. *Schellings Einfluss in der russischen Literatur.* Leipzig, 1939.

Varneke, B. V. *History of the Russian Theater.* New York, 1951.

von Gronicka, André. *The Russian Image of Goethe.* Philadelphia, 1968.

Winter, E. *Halle als Ausgangspunkt der deutschen Russlandkunde.* Berlin, 1953.

Zhirmunsky, V. *Gete v russkoy literature.* Leningrad, 1937.

Ziegengeist, G., ed. *I. S. Turgenjew und Deutschland.* Berlin, 1965.

CHAPTER 1: FYODOR SOLOGUB AND HEINRICH MANN

Primary Sources

Mann, Heinrich. *Gesammelte Romane.* 10 vols. Leipzig, 1917. Vol. VI.

———. *Macht und Mensch.* München, 1919.

———. *Die Göttinnen.* Berlin, 1932.

Sologub, Fyodor. *Sobranie sochineniy.* 13 vols. St. Petersburg, n. d.

———. *The Little Demon.* New York, 1916.

Secondary Sources

Boonstra, Pieter. *Heinrich Mann als politischer Schriftsteller.* Utrecht, 1945.

Chebotarevskaya, A., ed. *O. F. Sologube Kritika.* St. Petersburg, 1911.

Fechter, Paul. *Geschichte der deutschen Literatur.* Gütersloh, 1952.

Harkins, William E. *Dictionary of Russian Literature.* New York, 1956.

Hofman, Alois. *Thomas Mann und die Welt der russischen Literatur.* Berlin, 1967.

Ivanov, Vyacheslav. *Po zvezdam.* St. Petersburg, 1909.

Lo Gatto, Ettore. *Storia della letteratura russa.* Firenze, 1944.

Luther, Arthur. "Fedor Sologub," *Osteuropa* III (Berlin, 1927–28), 298–306.

Martini, Fritz. *Deutsche Literaturgeschichte.* Stuttgart, 1952.

Mirsky, D. S. *A History of Russian Literature.* New York, 1949.

Motylyova, T. "Leo Tolstoj und die deutsche Literatur," *Kunst und Literatur* XI–XII (Berlin, 1960), 1104–1116.

Neider, Charles, ed. *The Stature of Thomas Mann.* New York, 1947.

Poggioli, Renato. *The Poets of Russia.* Cambridge, Mass., 1960.

Schober, E. *Thomas Mann und Tolstoj.* Göttingen, 1950.

Sinsheimer, Hermann. *Heinrich Manns Werk.* München, 1921.

Tkhorzhevsky, Ivan. *Russkaya literatura.* Paris, 1950.

Venohr, L. *Thomas Manns Verhältnis zur russischen Literatur.* Meisenheim/Glan, 1959.

von Gronicka, André. "Thomas Mann and Russia," *The Stature of Thomas Mann,* ed. Charles Neider. New York, 1947. Pp. 307–25.

———. *Thomas Mann: Profile and Perspectives.* New York, 1970.

Weisstein, Ulrich. *Heinrich Mann: Eine historisch-kritische Einführung in sein dichterisches Werk.* Tübingen, 1962.

CHAPTER 2: MAKSIM GORKY

Primary Sources

Gorky, M. *Sobranie sochineniy.* 30 vols. Moskva, 1949–55.

Secondary Sources

Alekseyev, M. P., ed. *Mezhdunarodnye svyazi russkoy literatury.* Moskva, 1963.

Balukhaty, S. D. and Desnitsky, V. A., ed. *M. Gorky—Materialy i issledovania.* 4 vols. Moskva-Leningrad, 1936.

Brandt, Thomas. "Brecht und die Bibel," *PMLA* LXXIX (March 1964), 171–76.

Byalik, Boris A. *M. Gorky—literaturny kritik.* Moskva, 1960.

Czikowsky, E., et al., ed. *Maxim Gorki in Deutschland, Bibliographie 1899 bis 1965.* Berlin, 1968.

Ermolaev, Herman. *Maxim Gorky—Untimely Thoughts: Essays on Revolution, Culture and the Bolsheviks 1917–1918.* New York, 1968.

Gassner, John. *Masters of the Drama.* New York, 1954.

Idzikowski, Ilse. "Maxim Gorki in der DDR und in Westdeutschland," *Kunst und Literatur* XVI (1968), 3–18.

Lavretsky, A. *Esteticheskie vzglyady russkikh pisateley.* Moskva, 1963.

Ludwig, N. *Maxim Gorki.* Berlin, 1968.

Lukacs, Georg. *Der russische Realismus in der Weltliteratur.* 2 vols. Berlin, 1964.

Mikhaylovsky, B. V. *Tvorchestvo Gorkogo i mirovaya literatura.* Moskva, 1965.

Moravcevich, N. "Gorky and the Western Naturalists," *Comparative Literature,* XXI (1969), 63–75.

Peterson, Otto P. *Schiller in Russland.* New York, 1934.

Poggioli, Renato. *The Poets of Russia.* Cambridge, Mass., 1960.

Schiller, F. P. *Fridrikh Schiller.* Moskva, 1955.

Setschkareff, Vsevolod. *Geschichte der russischen Literatur.* Stuttgart, 1966.

Sheldon, Richard R. "Šklovskij, Gor'kij, and the Serapion Brothers," *SEEJ* XII (Spring 1968), 1–13.

Weil, Irwin. *Gorky.* New York, 1966.

Wolfe, B. D. *The Bridge and the Abyss: The Troubled Friendship of Maxim Gorky and V. I. Lenin.* New York, 1967.

Yuzovsky, Yu. *Maksim Gorky i yego dramaturgia.* Moskva, 1959.

CHAPTER 3: BLOK

Primary Sources

Pisma Aleksandra Bloka k rodnym, ed. M. A. Beketova. Leningrad, 1927.

Blok, Aleksandr. *Sobranie sochineniy.* 12 vols. Leningrad, 1936.

A. Blok i A. Bely—Perepiska, ed. V. N. Orlov. Moskva, 1940.

Blok, Aleksandr. *Sochinenia.* 2 vols. Moskva, 1955.

Gertsen (Herzen), A. I. *Polnoye sobranie sochineniy i pisem,* ed. M. K. Lemke. 22 vols. St. Petersburg, 1919–25.

Ivanov, Vyacheslav. *Po zvezdam.* Moskva, 1905.

Secondary Sources

Alekseyev, M. P., ed. *Mezhdunarodnye svyazi russkoy literatury.* Moskva, 1963.

Demtschenko and Genin. "Schiller auf den Bühnen des revolutionären Petrograd," *Sinn und Form* XI (Berlin, 1959), 927–935.

Donchin, G. *The Influence of French Symbolism on Russian Poetry.* 's-Gravenhage, 1958.

Ermatinger, Emil. *Deutsche Dichter.* 2 vols. Bonn, 1948.

Kluge, R. D. *Westeuropa & Russland im Weltbild Aleksandr Bloks.* München, 1967.

Laffitte, Sophie. *Alexandre Blok.* Paris, 1958.

Longyear, R. M. *Schiller and Music.* Chapel Hill, 1966.

Martini, F. *Deutsche Literaturgeschichte.* Stuttgart, 1952.

Orlov, V. N. *Aleksandr Blok.* Moskva, 1956.

Poggioli, Renato. *The Poets of Russia.* Cambridge, Mass., 1960.

Reeve, F. D. *Aleksandr Blok.* New York, 1962.

Robertson, J.G. *A History of German Literature.* New York, n.d.

Santoli, Vittorio. *Fra Germania e Italia.* Firenze, 1962.

Slonim, Marc. *Russian Theater.* Cleveland & New York, 1961.

von Gronicka, André. "Friedrich Schiller's Marquis Posa," *Germanic Review* XXVI (Oct. 1951), 196–214.

CHAPTER 4: BOTKIN

Primary Sources

Belinsky, V. G. *Pisma.* 3 vols. St. Petersburg, 1914.

———. *Polnoye sobranie sochineniy.* 13 vols. Moskva, 1953–59.

"Pisma V. G. Belinskogo i V. P. Botkina k A. A. Krayevskomu," *Otchet Imperatorskoy Publichnoy Biblioteki za 1889 g.* St. Petersburg, 1893. Prilozhenia.

Botkin, V. P. *Sochinenia V. P. Botkina.* 2 vols. St. Petersburg, 1890.

"Pisma V. P. Botkina," N. Izmaylov, ed. *Literaturnaya Mysl* II (Petrograd, 1923), 159–91.

V. P. Botkin i I. S. Turgenev—Neizdannaya perepiska. Moskva, 1930.

Grillparzer, Franz. *Sämtliche Werke,* W. Eichner, ed. 16 vols. Berlin, n. d.

Schillers Sämtliche Werke. Säkular-Ausgabe, 16 vols. Stuttgart & Berlin, n. d.

Stankevich—Perepiska, Aleksey Stankevich, ed. Moskva, 1914.

"Lettres inédites de L. Tolstoi a Botkine," J. W. Bienstock, ed. *Les oeuvres libres* (Paris, 1926), 5–36.

Secondary Sources

Annenkov, P. V. *Literaturnye vospominania.* Moskva, 1960.

Bolshaya Sovetskaya Entsiklopedia. Moskva, 1927. Vol. VII, 251.

———. Moskva, 1950. Vol. V, 642.

Bowman, H. *V. Belinski.* Cambridge, Mass., 1954.

Chizhevsky, D. *Gegel v Rossii.* Paris, 1939.

———. *Hegel bei den Slaven.* Bad Homburg, 1961.

Fet, A. *Moi vospominania.* 2 vols. Moskva, 1890.

Kostka, E. "At the Roots of Russian Westernism," *SEES* VI (Montreal, 1961), 158–76.

———. "Bakunin," *Monatshefte* LIV (March 1962), 109–16.

Lazursky, V. "V. P. Botkin," *Artist* XLIII (Moskva, 1894), 91–98.

Lozinskaya, L. *Schiller.* Moskva, 1960.

Lyaskovsky, A. *Martirolog russkikh pisateley.* Berlin, 1956.

Martini, F. *Deutsche Literaturgeschichte.* Stuttgart, 1952.

Mezhdunarodnye svyazi russkoy literatury, M. P. Alekseyev, ed. Moskva-Leningrad, 1963.

Pfeiffer, J. *Die deutsche Lyrik,* B. von Wiese, ed. 2 vols. Düsseldorf, 1959. Vol. II. 115–17.

Ryazanov, D. *Karl Marx i russkie ludi sorokovykh godov.* Petrograd, 1918.

Sakulin, P. N. *Russkaya literatura i sotsializm.* Moskva, 1922.

Schiller, F. P. *Fridrikh Schiller.* Moskva, 1955.

Setschkareff, W. *Schellings Einfluss in der russischen Literatur.* Leipzig, 1939.

Struve, P. *Na raznye temy.* St. Petersburg, 1902.

Varneke, B. V. *History of the Russian Theater.* New York, 1951.

Vetrinsky, Ch. "V. P. Botkin," *Novoye Slovo* XII (St. Petersburg, 1894), 39–105.

von Wiese, Benno, ed. *Die deutsche Lyrik.* Düsseldorf, 1959.

Zenkovsky, V. *A History of Russian Philosophy.* 2 vols. New York, 1953.

Zviguilsky, A. "V. P. Botkin chez Victor Hugo," *RLC* XXXIX (Paris, June 1965), 287–90.

CHAPTER 5: GRANOVSKY

Primary Sources

Belinsky, V. G. *Pisma.* 3 vols. St. Petersburg, 1914.

Gertsen (Herzen), A. I. *Polnoye sobranie sochineniy i pisem,* ed. M. K. Lemke. 22 vols. St. Petersburg, 1919–25.

T. N. Granovsky i yego perepiska. 2 vols. Moskva, 1897.

Sochinenia T. N. Granovskogo, ed. P. Kudryavtsev. Moskva, 1900.

Izbrannye sochinenia T. N. Granovskogo, ed. V. A. Sokolov. Moskva, 1905.

Ogarev, N. P. *Izbrannye sotsialno-politicheskie i filosofskie proizvedenia.* 2 vols. Moskva, 1952.

N. V. Stankevich—Perepiska, ed. Aleksey Stankevich. Moskva, 1914.

Secondary Sources

Asinovskaya, S. A. *Iz istorii peredovykh idei v russkoy medievistike.* Moskva, 1955.

———. *Lektsii T. N. Granovskogo po istorii srednevekovya.* Moskva, 1961.

Bolshaya Sovetskaya Entsiklopedia. Moskva, 1952. Vol XII.

Granovsky, T. N. Bibliography, ed. S. S. Dmitriyev. Moskva, 1969.

Lavrin, Janko. *Pushkin.* London, 1947.

Levshin, D. M. *N. Granovsky.* St. Petersburg, 1901.

Mann, Golo. *Geschichte und Geschichten.* Frankfurt, 1961.

Minayeva, N. V. *Granovsky v Moskve.* Moskva, 1963.

Schieder, Theodor. *Begegnungen mit der Geschichte.* Göttingen, 1962.

Schiller—Bicentenary Lectures, ed. F. Norman. London, 1960.

Schwab, Gustav B. *Schillers Leben.* Stuttgart, 1840.

Sidorov, N. "T. N. Granovsky," *Besedy.* Sbornik. Moskva, 1915.

Stender—Petersen, *Geschichte der Russischen Literatur* 2 vols. München, 1957.

Tkhorzhevsky, Ivan. *Russkaya literatura.* Paris, 1950.

Vetrinsky, Ch. *Gumanist 40–kh godov* (T. N. Granovsky). Moskva, 1905.

———. *T. N. Granovsky i yego vremya.* St. Petersburg, 1905.

von Gronicka, André. "Friedrich Schiller's Marquis Posa," *Germanic Review* XXVI (Oct. 1951), 196–214.

CHAPTER 6: PUSHKIN

Primary Sources

Belinsky, V. G. *Polnoye sobranie sochineniy.* 13 vols. Moskva 1953–59.

Blok, Aleksandr. *Sochinenia.* 2 vols. Moskva, 1955.

Dostoyevsky, F. *Polnoye sobranie sochineniy.* 14 vols. St. Petersburg, 1883–1904.

Milonov, M. V. *Sochinenia M. V. Milonova,* ed. A. Smirdin. St. Petersburg, 1849.

Pushkin, A. S. *Sochinenia A. S. Pushkina,* ed. P. O. Morozov. 7 vols. St. Petersburg, 1887.

———. *Sochinenia i pisma Pushkina,* ed. P. O. Morozov. 8 vols. St. Petersburg, 1903–05.

———. *Pushkin,* ed. S. A. Vengerov. Vols. I–III and IX. St. Petersburg, 1907–15.

———. *Pushkin—Pisma,* ed. B. L. Modzalevsky. 3 vols. Moskva-Leningrad, 1926–35.

———. *Sochinenia Pushkina,* ed. L. Maykov. Vols. I–IV, IX, XI. St. Petersburg, 1900–1929.

———. *Rukoyu Pushkina,* ed. M. A. Pavlovsky. Moskva-Leningrad, 1935.

———. *Polnoye sobranie sochineniy.* 20 vols. Moskva-Leningrad, 1937–49.

Schiller, ed. S. A. Vengerov. 4 vols. St. Petersburg, 1900.

Zhukovsky, V. A. *Stikhotvorenia.* Leningrad, 1956.

Secondary Sources

Bersano Begey, Marina. *Storia della letteratura polacca.* Milano, 1957.

Cheshikhin, V. *Zhukovsky kak perevodchik Schillera.* Riga, 1895.

Čyževskyj, D. "Schiller und die Brüder Karamasow," *Zeitschrift für*

Slawische Philologie VI (Leipzig, 1929), 1–42.

Ehrhard, M. *Joukovski et le pré-romantisme russe.* Paris, 1938.

Fischer, Rudolf. "Schiller und Puschkin," *Wissenschaftliche Zeitschrift der Karl Marx-Universität Leipzig* IX (Leipzig 1959–60), 73–76.

———. "Schiller und Puschkin," *Weimarer Beiträge* III (1960), 603–11.

fon Shteyn, Sergey. *Pushkin mistik.* Riga, 1931.

Gruzinsky, A. *Literaturnye ocherki.* Moskva, 1902.

Harder, H. B. *Schiller in Russland.* Bad Homburg, 1969.

Kostka, E. *Schiller in Russian Literature.* Philadelphia, 1965.

Kropotkin, P. *Ideals and Realities in Russian Literature.* New York, 1925.

Lavrin, Janko. *Pushkin and Russian Literature.* London, 1947.

Lo Gatto, Ettore. *Puškin.* Milano, 1959.

Ostafyevsky Arkhiv Knyazey Vyazemskikh. St. Petersburg, 1899, Vol. II[1].

Peterson, O. P. *Schiller in Russland.* New York, 1934.

Pushkin v mirovoy literature. Sbornik. Leningrad, 1926.

Pushkin—kritik, ed. N. V. Bogoslovsky. Moskva, 1950.

Pushkin i yego sovremenniki. St. Petersburg, 1913.

Pushkinskaya yubileynaya literatura 1899–1900, ed. V. Sipovsky. St. Petersburg, 1902.

Rozova, Z. "Pushkin i 'Idealy' Schillera," *Slavia,* XIV (Prague, 1936–37), 384–88.

Russkie pisateli 19-go veka o Pushkine, ed. A. S. Dolinin. Leningrad, 1938.

Santoli, Vittorio. *Storia della letteratura tedesca.* Firenze, 1967.

Schiller, ed. S. A. Vengerov. 4 vols. St. Petersburg, 1900.

Setschkareff, V. *Geschichte der russischen Literatur.* Stuttgart, 1966.

Shaw, J. Thomas. "Recent Soviet Scholarly Books on Puškin," *SEEJ* X (Spring 1966), 66–84.

Tomashevsky, B. *Pushkin.* Moskva-Leningrad. 2 vols. Moskva-Leningrad, 1956 and 1961.

Troyat, Henri. *Pushkin.* New York, 1950.

Varneke, B. V. *History of the Russian Theatre.* New York, 1951.

Veselovsky, Yury, "Schiller kak vdokhnovitel russkikh pisateley," *Russkaya Mysl,* II (Moskva, 1906), 1–15.

Vladimirsky, G. D. "Pushkin—perevodchik," *Pushkin,* IV–V. Moskva-Leningrad, 1939.

Volm, M. *W. A. Zhukovskij als Übersetzer* Ann Arbor, Michigan, 1945.

von Gronicka, André. "Lermontov's Debt to Goethe," *RLC* XL (Winter 1966), 567–84.

———. *The Russian Image of Goethe.* Philadelphia, 1968.

von Wiese, Benno. *Friedrich Schiller.* Stuttgart, 1963.

Index